Who Are *You* Calling *Grandma?*

True Confessions of a Baby Boomer's Passage

Maridel Bowes, M.A.

3L Publishing
Sacramento, California

Who Are You Calling Grandma?
True Confessions of A Baby Boomer's Passage

3L Publishing books may be ordered through booksellers or by contacting:
3lpublishing.com

Because of the dynamic nature of the Internet,
any Web addressesor links contained in this book may have
changed since publication and may no longer be valid.

ISBN: 978-1-4276-4021-5

Printed in the United States of America

For Sandi

*for always encouraging me
to talk to my Wise Woman
and
for being the Wisest Woman I Know*

Contents

Acknowledgments.. v

Foreword.. vii

Introduction ix

The First Trimester 1

Second Trimester.. 21

Third Trimester 73

Epilogues... 129

Afterward... 131

Acknowledgments

To my Mom, Addie Woodcook, who at 88 is still a class act and in a class by herself. Thank you for a lifetime of love and belief.

To Justin, who made me both a mother and a grandmother. The sound of your children's laughter at play with you is the most beautiful music in my world. As a father, you are an amazing combination of strong commitment and genuine playfulness. I love you.

To Nikki, daughter of my heart. As this book so clearly shows, our relationship is a rarity! I am blessed to have you as the mother of my grandchildren, as they are blessed to have you for their mother.

To Gavin, my son and spiritual guide. Your wise, loving spirit pervades my life whether you are looking in my eyes or are half-way across the world.

To Donna, whose heart of gold and open door policy have given me another reason to love and visit Portland. I cherish our evolving relationship as mutually-adopted mother and daughter.

To Sandi, beloved friend and companion on the journey. So much of my inner strength and trust in the Process is because of your living, loving presence. Thank you for your unfailing support of my teaching and writing for the last 20 years. This one is for you.

To Johnnie, "The Dancin Man," who brought fabulous music, wild laughter and swing dance into my quiet life. Your love, playfulness and soulfulness have forever expanded the horizons of my heart.

To Margaret, my dear friend and dedicated editor. My heartfelt thanks for your exotic blend of enthusiasm, honesty, and command of the English language.

To Michelle Gamble-Risley, marketer extraordinaire and comrade of the heart. Thank you for helping me reinvent, rejuvenate and realize my "Second Bloom" life.

To Erin Pace for your "graphic influence" on my work, your sweet disposition and the exceptional beauty of this book from cover to cover.

To Dale Kolke for using your camera and your talented eye to make me look like one hot Grandma.

And lastly, to person who started me on this journey …

My first grandchild, the dearest of hearts. I wouldn't have missed you for the whole wide world.

Foreword

Browsing through bookstores, I always avoid picking up those books about preparing for the important *passages of life.* You know the titles I'm talking about. I can't name them right now because there is something in me that has always resisted the whole concept of preparing for special events in our lives the way we'd prepare for a trip overseas.

It's probably vanity on my part, and no doubt has something to do with resisting the idea that time passes and we age. But I have convinced myself there's more to my resistance than that. I'd like to think I'm in touch with this higher intelligence that allows me to dodge the harsher realities of life. Psychologists have a name for this, of course: denial. Years ago, I read some research someone did, looking for something that all successful men and women shared. It turns out that the one personal trait they all had in common was denial. That's right; they were all great at putting out of their minds anything that troubled them. My therapists—I've had several throughout my life—have always tried to convince me that denial is a bad thing, that if I ever hoped to live a happy and fulfilling life I'd have to give it up. However, I'm still not fully convinced of that.

Reading this book, however, I found that Maridel held up a mirror to my psyche that has at least made me question some of my assumptions. My reading came at a time when my son had started complaining that I was really—how can I put this?—falling down in my duties as a grandfather. And I have to confess he had a point. I'd never gotten into this *doting* thing, as in "doting grandfather." It isn't that I don't love my grandkids; I truly do. But, well, I simply wasn't ready for that reality yet. I don't do *dote*. And, okay, I may have been in denial about growing older.

However, reading Maridel Bowes' manuscript did something for me I wasn't counting on. It made me look, and it made me laugh, first *with* her and then *at* myself. And it was fun! It turned out to be the most pleasant and most emotionally productive trip through denial I ever could have imagined. Like me, Maridel knows how to do denial really well. She paints a vivid picture of her expertise in that area, particularly around the news that she was going to be a grandmother. I won't give away the whole story, or even hint at how she did or didn't get to a place of accepting the reality of her grandmotherhood, because the most important truth revealed in these pages isn't whether she did or didn't, but the sparkle of the process itself.

Don't get me wrong. I still defend denial as a great gift. But as painful as it is for me to admit, there are some experiences in life that are better off without it. As entertaining and funny as this book is, the journey Maridel shares here transcends its own comedy and, if you're paying attention at all, will deliver you closer to that famous place that wisdom keepers call *the now*.

Hal Zina Bennett,
Write From the Heart: Unleashing the Power of Your Creativity

Introduction

It seems that neither my grandchild nor I have been born yet.

Of course, Baby has the perfect excuse: there are still eight weeks to hang out in Hotel Uteriné before nature declares check-out time. My own excuse is neither as mystical nor as legit. It's simply this: I never thought of myself as a grandma. I suppose such astounding lack of foresight has something to do with wanting to maintain my youth—or at least the latest version of it. But I really don't think that's the heart of the matter. For me it's more fundamental than that (and here I must resort to a confessional tone): *I'm just not sure I'm grandma material.* In fact, I have this nagging suspicion that I could be missing the Grangene altogether. At least this is my excuse for having a daughter-in-law who's seven months pregnant while I have yet to fully conceive of myself as a grandmother.

So at two months and counting, here's the implausible state of things: At this very moment, the Anticipated One is two time zones away, enrolled in the pre-school of humanity, sucking thumb while mother snorkels, and kicking up bony little heels while she attempts to relax on the Kohala Coast. Meanwhile, I am happily land-locked, house and doggie sitting for the expectant pair while they perform the last rites of a (nearly) child free vacation—without of course, fully comprehending the nature of their indulgence.

I'm in and out of their house all day—tending to the dogs, meandering the funky aisles of the independent grocery, briskly walking the hilly surround, deep-watering the flower beds—and yet, when I'm behind closed doors, I'm drawn again and again to the little lamb and gingham paradise that sits at the end of the hall. Some part of me seems convinced that if I linger here long enough, I'll come to accept the startling and incomprehensible fact that very soon, I'm going to be someone's ... someone's ... that my son and his wife are having a baby.

I assure you, the situation isn't so bad that my children insisted I come sit in the nursery until I could act like a decent grandmother. Actually I *volunteered* to come dog sit, which given my disposition toward canines, stops just this side of noble. Okay, so I'm fond of these *particular* dogs, got complimentary plane fare, and an eight-day-seven-night breather from my chronically cranky to-do lists (you can never please them), but I still count my choice as progress. It seems radically similar to something a bona fide grandmother-in-waiting might do. But maybe the truth is that I simply came to sit—not only with the backyard beasts (as my son affectionately calls them), or in front of the curiously comforting wiles of HGTV, but here in this house, in this little corner room bursting with unused promise. Perhaps I came, after all, to sit in the nursery chair my mother and I bought, and rock myself into a new existence.

Like every crucial passage since the age of twenty-seven, this one too has brought me to my journal, which is the writer's equivalent of being brought to her knees. You have to tell the truth on your knees. Otherwise, why bother? A journal is just like that. It's a little spiral-bound altar where the words get soft and sticky when you start to lie to yourself. Then the pen starts hovering over the page, and inevitably, the doodling begins. Only honesty can save you from the ill repute of doodling. People in my grandfather's church hailed him as the Prayer Warrior because he had cracks in his shoes from kneeling so much. I do sometimes get stiff fingers from bending over my little blue-lined altar, which doesn't play quite as well as splitting shoes. But as long as I can avoid the margins, I figure I'm on the right path.

～ა◯

So that's what I'm attempting to do as the unyearned-for mantle of the *third generation* falls to me: trying to keep from marginalizing this moment. Trying to stay instead with my real-me experience of it—even if it is about as flattering as last decade's swim suit.

Of course, I gather my imagined comrades around me. I tell myself that I can't be the only fifty-something woman who never tried that hard to envision herself as a grandmother—and who got so easily distracted when she did. "Surely my misgivings aren't just mine," I mutter as I prepare to wedge myself into these strange new shoes, like some aging stepsister of Cinderella. Speaking of shoes, I wonder if *Grandmother-hood* might be one of the last stomping grounds of having it Our Way. One of the last re-inventions in the Boomer Do-It-Yourself Kit. I suspect that as with everything else, we'll turn the stomping into a dance, recreating what we don't relate to, remaking it in our own image. And in the process, believing we've made it better.

So this is my two-step, my bit in the greater dance: the journal of a woman in the throes of becoming a grandmother. Missing gene or not.

Maridel Bowes
Dillon Beach, California
2003

The First Trimester

Freud Cringes From Beyond the Grave

November 29

My daughter, Nikki, was birthed to me in a wedding gown and a dazzling smile at the age of twenty: a gift from my firstborn son. Five years later, as she drives me to the airport after My-Turn-to-Share-the-Turkey visit, she's waxing eloquent about the projected three year plan: building careers, getting debts paid off, possibly buying a bigger house. My son is almost thirty and ready for a child, but she's diligently making her mark in the world and both she and the world are impressed. I sympathize with my son, but I'm glad she's giving herself time to flourish, to make friends with her competence. And neither do I mind the fact that she's giving me an extended warranty on my middle age. I smile smugly as we speed along in the night. Her bio-clock is no doubt ticking away somewhere inside, but evidently no one has set the alarm yet.

In just three days that starlit ride and its moonstruck prattle will seem incredibly naïve. And the two of us will seem like a pair of little chatty ostriches that can't imagine how we got so much sand in our eyes. For one thing, during most of my visit, she'd been complaining of pain in her breasts, especially when she exercised. Okay, that could have multiple causes. But for another, she'd confided in me that she was over a week late. Well, that's happened before. But here's the clincher: after mapping out the gestalt of the next three years, she'd seamlessly transitioned into projecting family stats. "Just think, if I got pregnant tonight, I'd be thirty-six when the child was ten. And Justin would be almost forty. And if got pregnant again a couple of years from now, we'd be married eighteen years by the time that child was ten."

Ahhh yes, the unconscious having the last word.

And that's exactly what should have alerted me: that sudden, illogical shift that in the blink of an eye, shot down her three-year plan. I was a psychotherapist for fifteen years for God's sake. Freud would hang his one-track head.

December 1

Nikki calls to talk about sticks. The kind inside pregnancy kits. Now, of course, I've never used a pregnancy kit. I've only seen the commercials, and therefore I don't trust them. (Ever since I stopped up sewer lines with tampons years ago and had a plumber tell me "not to believe Madison Avenue," I've been appropriately wary.) Besides, a lined stick vs. an un-lined stick has never enthralled me as a way to enter life's most mysterious relationship. So Nikki and I giggle together, home phone to cell phone, about those things "being wrong all the time," although I realize afterward that I'd been doing most of the giggling. And some time later, I remembered that all the other times she'd taken those tests of which I'm so suspicious, they'd been absolutely accurate. In fact, they'd been right *every* time so far. Still, isn't there something about false positives being more common than false negatives—or is it the other way around?

December 3

Two kits (of different brands) later and now the stick is giggling. In fact, all three of them are laughing behind their little blue lines. Nikki's convinced it's definitive. Of course she's not from the generation that believes it's only official if you've been *pronounced* pregnant by a lab technician who's had an up close and personal moment with your urine, and in turn, by an M.D. in a white coat, lab results in hand. Actually, I no longer ascribe to such formalities. In my heart, I believe a woman can know she's pregnant with nothing but the x-ray vision of instinct. But today I regress. I'm not ready to look the rather bawdy truth in the eye.

Expectant Grandmother Braves Ocean in Dinghy

December 5

Even with the doctor's appointment a couple of days away, it seems clear that we are about to be launched onto the great wide ocean of HavingABaby. Justin and Nikki appear to have already made themselves seaworthy. He is exuberant, a man who doesn't waste enthusiasm on every little thing and therefore has plenty to lavish on things that matter. She seems a bit more dazed, but has hopped aboard and is waving back at me as they put out to sea. I'm in my own little dinghy—not quite prepared, not quite believing, and not doing much paddling. At the moment I am mostly happy for them, putt-putting along on the fumes of their joy.

Tonight I lay in bed and wondered about the efficacy of being so happy for people who have no idea what they're in for. No one in a state of prenatal euphoria has any idea of the river they've just stepped into. And no way to know. Regardless of whether the venture goes all the way to the North Star or as south as south can go, they simply have no idea what it means to have a piece of yourself living and breathing in someone else's body. Still, I can't and won't relinquish my joy for them. Partly because there's wisdom in innocence and partly because right now, it's the only thing I feel.

December 7

It's officially, medically, absolutely so. Nikki and Justin are expecting their first child. My firstborn is the expectant father of his firstborn. Life cycles 'round. I wish I felt deliriously happy, the way my mother felt when Justin was conceived. It's not that I'm *un*happy, but neither am I tossing back champagne or calling my ten best friends (of which, in truth there are only three). Nikki seemed to sense my lack of zest when they called tonight. "It's just so unexpected!" I told her gaily, but I knew she could hear through it. She always can.

December 10

I entered the great cathedral of Barnes and Noble today. Truly, for a place of such unmitigated commerce, it somehow evokes that hushed, holy feeling in me. I swear that some part of me genuflects every time I pass through the electronic portals. Maybe it's those weighty, impressive double doors that invoke a sense of reverence. Or perhaps it's the intoxicating incense from the adjoining temple of Starbucks. I only know that once inside, cup in hand, I'm ready to worship.

Today, however, is different. I head directly for the information desk to make my baby-specific query. I was led to, not pointed-in-the-direction-of, the precise and desired shelf. My obliging assistant even took the time to pull out a popular selection for me. I thanked her, flipped through it, and promptly returned it to its slot. I'm looking for the book that I wish I'd had as a neo-natalphyte. A book that describes the day-by-day developments of fetal progress. Day 26: aorta begins to form! Day 72: migrating intestines! Day 131: heartbeat audible through a stethoscope! The book the employee offered me was too graphic, too journalistically honest in its portrayal of Day 270 or thereabouts. I leave that level of revelation to the hearty medical types (God bless them) who run birthing classes and whose sensibilities aren't shattered by living color. For the moment, I want to stay within the blurred lines of the developing mystery, within that almost unfathomable realm of ear buds and translucent eyelids. A few more tries and the perfect book finds its way into my grasp: *The Pregnancy Journal* by Christine Harris. Its day-by-day format provides minimal, inviting space for the newly pregnant to record her thoughts and feelings. And most importantly, that space is surrounded by ordered and delicate descriptions of the deepest mystery known to man and womankind.

December 14

Nikki and Justin had their first doctor appointment and without warning, an image of the six-week-old fetus popped onto the screen, compliments of a vaginal ultrasound. (There's a part of me that thinks even less of a vaginal ultrasound than it does of lines on a stick. And the other part of me is as jealous as a jade-eyed cat. But my reaction is exceedingly beside the point here.) That sudden, unexpected image plugged Nikki into the living matrix of motherhood. She's no longer just a woman who simply knows she's pregnant. That knowledge has now slipped from head to gut and landed in the soft bed of instinct. "All of a sudden it was real!" she told me, sounding like a love-struck schoolgirl. "I can't begin to tell you how I feel. How different it all is!" She didn't have to. Her joy tap-danced across the phone lines and clicked its heels in rhythm with my heart.

When the phone was passed to Justin, I once again heard the elation in his voice, heightened by impact of the ultrasound. A copy of the life-altering image is already posted on their fridge. I tried to picture it: a snapshot of their barely-conceived child hanging there in the midst of magnets and mug shots, just to the left of their whiteboard scribbled with the minutiae of daily living. They can see their baby now. S/he's already settled into the cheery bedlam of their refrigerator life. But I can't see this babe at all yet. I can't even imagine what such an image would look like. Or what I'll feel when I see it.

"So I just need to find my own excitement," I tell my companion Sandi that night. "Without the aid of technology."

"Or hormones," she added dryly. Tonight I stood in front of the mirror and gazed at my vibrant, smiling, still-capable-of-being-sexy-self and said, "Hey kid, I know you're not going to believe this, but you're going to be … one of *them*."

This is one of the unique problems of my generation, I thought as I tucked myself into bed. Many of us don't see Grandmotherhood as natural. Well, that's not quite true. We see it as natural for our grandmothers. Yes, sure, we wanted grandmothers. And we see it as natural for our mothers. Yes, sure, we wanted our children to have grandmothers. But somehow, the logic of the next step failed to occur to some of us. Grandmothers were *them* and we weren't waiting around for our turn, knitting and dreaming and dropping hints. So while in some abstract way we would wish our theoretical grandchildren to have theoretical grandmothers, we didn't necessarily want to *be* them. At least not yet.

It seems that Yet has not only arrived on my humble doorstep, but is ready to elbow its way over my threshold. I'm not ready tonight, but soon, I'll be stepping aside.

December 15

Newly-expectant parents have a strange case of boredom. More like boredomitis. They're officially pregnant and these days, they have baby's first photo op to prove it. But the next doctor's appointment is a month off and it's too early to do any worthwhile shopping. Their lives have been radically, inextricably altered and yet, unless you count morning sickness, nothing has visibly changed.

Which is where the search for the perfect name comes in. Every time I ring Portland a new name has wheedled its way to the top of the list. Sometimes even in the same phone call, a prospective daughter can go from Lauren to Hannah depending on which expectant parent has me on the line. Alexis was the short-lived favorite of both of them until Nikki dropped back to Lauren and set up camp. Justin also speaks of male names: Patrick, Logan, Quincy. Nikki treats boys' names like write-in candidates. Since she's from a family of girls, she blithely reasons, *what else would she have?* Such reasoning bespeaks her preference. "But I'll love this baby just as much if it's a boy, Mom. You know that." And I do know it. Nikki is a young woman of strong preferences and opinions. But she's even stronger on loving what belongs to her.

Ex-therapist Verges on Neurotic Breakdown

December 18

I'm definitely deranged. Right alongside a reluctance to claim my reproductive birthright is this full-blown neurotic inquiry: *"Who gets the baby next Christmas?!"* I know this is irrational. It's beyond irrational. There's probably some official diagnosis for such a serious split of psyche, but the problem is, whatever its classification, I'm stuck with it. No, I'm crazy with it.

I'm aware that up until this time I've drafted my tale as if Nikki had no family to speak of. In the reader's mind, perhaps, she was early-orphaned or the product of a family that had gone round the dysfunctional bend. Or at the very least one that lived across the country in some novel-worthy state of estrangement. None of these, however, is a representative sample of the truth. It's just that I just thought I'd give myself a running start, give the reader a glimpse of how exceptionally close I am to my daughter-by-marriage before I diluted the story with reality—which is that she's much closer to her own mother.

Nikki's family is more traditional than ours. Her parents, Ginny and Sam, are still married and own their own business. Her sister and husband live within shouting distance of the homestead and also prime the pump of the family trade. They are hard-working, loving, prosperous people whose preference would be to have Nikki and Justin live close by too. And while they seem to have made peace with the four-hour trek that separates them, as you might expect, these are folks that cherish Christmas with their family.

I've never personally spoken with my laws-in-law (coining as I go here) about our holiday arrangements, though it's become apparent that they would prefer to have each and every Christmas with their family intact. In the early years of Nikki and Justin's marriage, things seemed to be migrating in that direction, but have since evolved into an equitable arrangement: the families in question alternate Thanksgiving and Christmas celebrations from year-to-year. But now I have this funny feeling. I'm wondering if a first grandchild will break the spell of our unspoken agreement and automatically qualify them for the Intact Family All Rights Reserved Award.

So here I am—God help me—not wanting to admit that I'm a grandmother-in-the-making and *at the same time,* going nuts over the thought that my first Christmas with this baby might be revoked! Because next year will be, after all, Our Turn. ("Our" referring to my former husband and his wife, who live just a mile from me.) I realize that this is the kind of thing that drives people into therapy. In fact, it's the kind of thing that once-upon-a-time drove people into therapy with me as their therapist. I repeat, God help me. And since I spent so many years assuring clients that my real job was to help them become their own therapists, it seems I'm stuck with myself. Although I do frequently contract out. Sandi, who works as an analyst for the state, is one of the best therapists I've ever met. She just didn't bother getting that pesky degree. My friend Margaret is another consistent source of solid reflection. And despite her generous claims, she didn't learn it all from me. Lastly, my younger son Gavin rounds out Team Therapy. As fortune would have it, I'm scheduled to meet him downtown in a few days to deliver Christmas gifts to our Adopt-A-Family. In my condition, I'm reluctant to use the word *needy* in their behalf.

December 20

I've had my first sip of non-vicarious prenatal joy. I've just sent Christmas presents to Nikki and Justin that compensate for my weak response to the heir unapparent. My inspiration was a little cloth bag someone made when Justin was born, one of the few things I've saved. It's orange with green piping and bears an appliqué clown with all of the pertinent birth data cross-stitched upon his multi-colored balloons. It's still in excellent condition so I gently hand washed it and placed a few things inside: first, my own pink-striped pregnancy record book with an expectant bear on the cover and all my doctor visits, weight gains, and gift lists meticulously noted inside. Next, a paperback entitled *50 Ways to Tell If Your Baby is A Boy or A Girl.* It's full of simple tests from various cultures and though it emanates mostly from the Old Wives circuit, I thought it might be a distraction from The Perfect Name fixation. (Update: Nikki's not budging from Lauren, which Justin doesn't care for. He keeps coming back to Quincy for a boy which she will agree to under no circumstances. Her favorite male name, when she momentarily concedes it could be a boy: Ryan.) And lastly, I put a book in the bag that I read some years ago and desperately wished I'd read as a pregnant mother. Though in all honesty, I can't guarantee it would have interested me then. It's entitled, "The Secret Life of the Unborn Child," and when I visit Portland in January, I will reread it from my new and improved vantage point of thirty years.

One final offering from my small cache of memorabilia: a necklace. I felt a genuine trill of inspiration as I pulled it from my vintage-only jewelry box. You know the kind of box I mean. Mine is gold leatherette and houses, among other ludicrous treasures, my tarnished high school charm bracelet. (Three things are true about this bracelet: I'll never wear it again. It is of no value to anyone else. And I'll never part with it.) Hold on! Revelation! Maybe it's something a granddaughter would love! Or is that just so last century, playing dress-up with your grandmother's charm bracelet? Anyway, the opal necklace, our baby's birthstone, was the present my husband, Brad, gave me on the day Justin was born. Though I haven't worn it for years, I did of course commit it to the rest home for beloved old jewelry. So in the spirit of the times, I decided to pass it on. After purchasing a new chain for it, I had it made into an anklet for Nikki. I don't know if she'll love it, or even if she'll wear it. But passing on this piece of myself, this memento of my history as a mother, brings a quiet spark of connection to the next generation.

Only one thing remains now in my dresser drawer of keepsakes: a little yellow two-piece suit with a white, ribbed yoke circled by Scottie dogs. It was Justin's birth present from his Daddy. It's been double plastic-bagged all these years and appears to be in remarkably good condition. Chromosomes are even now deciding its fate. This morning I put everything in the mail and for the rest of the day, my heartburn ruminations about next Christmas nodded off like a colicky baby who unexpectedly graces you with sleep.

Woman Gives Birth to Own Therapist

December 23

After delivering baskets and boxes to our adopted families, Gavin and I settle into one of our favorite downtown haunts, The Tower Café. The food here is distinctly Californian and the atmosphere so full of bustle and clang that it creates its own version of privacy. I usually prefer something more environmentally subtle when dining out—but not when I'm downtown. After assessing our first-year experience with the Adopt-A-Family program, we turn to *my* current lack. Of peace.

Gavin listens thoughtfully as I pour out my angst. "And to top it all off," I say, eyeing a strolling Santa and hoping he won't interrupt my tabletop counseling session, "having the family together for Christmas isn't that easy for me anyway. For starters, I know Nikki would rather be with her family, which is always hard. And that's compounded by the growing disparity among us about gift-giving. Not to mention the fact that my stomach keeps track of everyone's mood. So when we're together, I end up feeling like the motherboard through which all circuits run."

"But the last thing you want is for it to be taken away," he says without a hint of mockery.

"Exactly!"

"I don't think losing Christmas together is really your biggest concern, Mom. I think you're more afraid of not feeling equal."

The proverbial nail just got hammered into the motherboard. Sparks fly, circuits fuse. Tears sting my eyes. (I hate crying in public, but perhaps my tears will at least ward off Santa.) I'd known all along there was something bigger beneath the surface. There always is when I'm secretly starring in a drama of my worst fears.

"I don't *feel* equal though. Nikki's parents live closer, they have more money, they're still together …"

He merely nods, knowing it's not the time for a swing vote toward optimism.

"I feel ridiculous! I'm so ambivalent about becoming a grandmother, and at the same time, afraid I'm going to miss a chance to be one."

"You'll get the chance. Maybe not in certain prescribed ways, but the big chance—the one all of us have, you know? The chance to know this child and have this child know you."

This is why I no longer have to pay for therapy.

As our food is served, something inside me relaxes with the truth. Still, I'm not so naïve as to imagine that the truth now chiming in my heart like Christmas bells, will effect a complete cure. I know that fears still lurk of being the lesser grandma. The California one. The Thanksgiving one. The one without a grandpa. It's just that for the moment, I remember that those fears are just fears, not spells cast by the Reality Witch. I'm also aware, however, that this shiny new perspective implies a certain emotional security on my part. And like my aging blood pressure, such security, I've found, all depends on the day you're checking levels.

When I take Gavin home, I get out of the car and we hug with celebratory gusto in the middle of the street. Tomorrow is officially Christmas. But in my heart, it's all taking place this moment on 27th Avenue in downtown Sacramento, where life and cold and the gift of intimacy-opened, pulse in the air around us. On the way back to the suburbs, I continue the conversation. Just me talking to me now about what I do want instead of what I don't. Me talking to me about the relationship I can have with this child regardless of distance, means, or my own misgivings. One of my old loves taught me that *quality* of relationship transcends all other amenities of life, and I silently thank him for leaving that gift in my care.

On the ride from the restaurant, Gavin and I had spoken of creating a whole new version of Christmas, a new tradition shaped by everyone's thoughts and desires. Now I realize that we already have our focal point. Never mind that we know neither name nor gender. Anything we create will be centered around this child—his needs, his naptime, his year-to-year changes. Or hers. And eventually, I'm sure, *theirs*.

Then, suddenly, a flashback induces an irrepressible grin: Justin at fourteen months, twirling in the paper and ribbon refuse of Christmas, absolutely high on color and crinkle.

A focal point indeed.

Christmas Day

I found an unmarked envelope tucked into my Christmas presents from Nikki and Justin. I knew what was inside: a copy of the image that had turned Nikki into a devotee of motherhood in one moment of technological wonder. Would it have the same magical effect on me, exposing in an instant the error of my diffident ways? Or perhaps, in order of concerns, would I even recognize what I was looking at? Or will I be forced to consult Sandi's keen eye for a first, meaningful glimpse of my progeny? I open the envelope slowly, my heart working up a little drum roll for the occasion. I see it all right: white etching on a field of black, a little cocoon that's bursting out of its own boundaries. I study it from various angles in an attempt to see *which way it goes,* but decide it's too soon to tell. The picture isn't alive for me the way it was for Justin and Nikki. "I guess you had to be there," I say softly, and put it on the fridge. Perhaps in the weeks ahead as I put away the soy milk or pull out the almond butter, the image will grow on me. No, the cockles of my heart aren't strangely-warmed, but I linger anyway, a finger on the tiny spot.

Our little morph.

December 27

Justin flew into town today. He's a regular at his high school's annual alumni vs. varsity basketball game. My former husband, Brad, and his wife, Cindy, are out of town for the holidays, so I am the lone family rep at the game. I wasn't the ideal private school mother in the years of my sons' Waldorf education. With great enthusiasm and relative promptness, I attended every school program or performance in which they participated. But I didn't do field trips or camping trips. Nor did I volunteer to run a chili booth at the annual Harvest Fair. Brad did all of that and more, God love him. My choice back then was to put every extra ounce of energy I had into finding out *who in the world* lay buried beneath the shellac of my conditioned self. But when it came to basketball, I was part of the scene. Brad and I went to every game, joining the pack of parents that roamed from one private school to another on Friday and Saturday nights. At basketball games, I belonged. I was Number 5's mother, proud of his passing prowess, the fakes before the shots, and his steady sportsmanship. It's been a decade now, however, and I no longer remember the names of the familiar faces that walk by, though we wave and nod from afar. Some of those I knew best aren't among the throng tonight, and I find myself wishing that Brad and Cindy were here to keep "lone" from becoming "lonely."

All that changes, of course, when Justin takes the floor. I clap and cheer, my muscles tensing when the ball leaves his hands, my voice whooping when it hits the mark and sighing when it doesn't. As I walk out into the moonlight after the game, this twinkling thought occurs to me: if your firstborn can transport you just that quickly after almost thirty years, a first grandchild must have charms beyond imagining.

December 29

Tonight Gavin sojourned from his downtown habitat to spend the night in the burbs with Justin and me. His preferred mode of transportation is the city bus, so we sit in the rain and dark waiting for friendly monster eyes to swing around the corner and come to a whooshing, creaturely stop before depositing our passenger from its well-lit innards. The three of us go to the neighborhood Mexican restaurant for dinner, where the subject of baby names arises as naturally as the steam off the tamales. Justin has backed off on Quincy, perhaps in the hope of getting Nikki to relinquish her grip on Lauren. "Logan" is currently at the top of the list for a boy's name, with the quirky bonus that Logan is the name of the street they live on.

"Hey, maybe we're starting a family tradition here," I say brightly. "Gavin's middle name is Taylor, which was the name of the street Dad and I lived on as newlyweds."

"Guess I better be careful where I live," Gavin says, smiling.

"So what do you think of the name Logan?" Justin asks his brother.

"I don't really care for it," he replies, "It somehow reminds me of log."

I admire his candidness. It's still hard for me to say flat out to someone I love that I don't like what they've expressed an affinity for. But actually, I do like the name Logan—though perhaps not as well as I did yesterday. When it had yet to remind me of log.

On Christmas Eve day, after our Tower Café counseling session, Gavin and I had stopped by the cigar shop next door. I'd purchased a cognac cigar for his stocking and another called Chocolate Thunder to share with his brother. At midnight tonight, just as I got into bed, the two of them stood on the porch, not far from my window, talking and passing the smoky torch between them. It's one of those moments you'd love to bottle, a moment all the more cherished because you can't. I drifted off to sleep wrapped in the sound of rain and the low rumble of my sons' voices, voices that arced now and then in laughter. And though I know better, I swear I could smell the sweet smoke of chocolate.

December 30

Justin left today, but not without leaving behind the gentle, palpable throb of his happiness. It was so visible in his eyes when he talked about the baby, like a high voltage glimmer he'd been saving for fatherhood. The proverbial gleam, I suppose. I only know that when I think of the baby now, I see Justin's face and hear the lilt in his voice. And for the first time it occurs to me that I can stop trying to feel like a grandma. Right now I only need to feel like a mother whose child is being reborn.

Expectant Grandma Spurns Honorific

January 1

Here's my New Year's resolution: I don't want to be called "Grandma."

"Grandma" is my father's mother, a tiny woman who bore six children and a hard life on a dairy farm in upstate New York. She was married to my grandfather of praying fame, who when he wasn't putting creases in his shoes, filled in for God—mostly the Old Testament version. So there wasn't a lot of space in grandma Pearl's life to demonstrate the spunk that aunts and uncles alluded to in an off-handed way, giving me the feeling that even as adults, they knew better than to make a point of it in front of Pa. But even I got a glimpse of it now and then. "Oh, hush, Merle," she'd say when his ribbing went too far. And miraculously, sometimes he did just that. Those moments notwithstanding, my impression of her has survived: a woman worn down by hard work, lifelong lack, and Pa. Even her faith seemed tired.

"Grandma" is also my mother's mother, Lizzie, who lived with my grandfather at the top of a long, steep hill in the river town of Beacon, New York. In contrast to Pearl, she was so large-boned and full of faith that she could inadvertently knock you over with her dogma. Lizzie was principled beyond all reason. She may have suffered for her faith, but other people suffered for it more. Even my brother and I, whom she pulled from the car each summer before it came to a full stop, didn't escape the long arm of her martyrdom. One summer, despite the stifling humidity, I asked in eight-year-old earnestness what she wanted for Christmas. She was riffling through the piano bench clutter, looking for a piece of sheet music. She turned to consider the question and me. "Oh, honey, I may not even be here by Christmas," she said with pitch-perfect sanctity, then mopped her brow with one of her limp, embroidered hankies, and returned to her search. Nearby, my mother gasped and rolled her eyes.

It's obvious that I never lived close to either of my grandmothers, geo-graphically or emotionally. And only once do I remember feeling truly grandmothered. It was the Christmas that Grandma Lizzie went out on a limb for me. I was five and wanted a life-size baby doll. She worked at Schoonmaker's Department Store downtown, and with the help of layaway and an employee discount, could get a much nicer doll than my parents could manage. Her next-door neighbor, Ray Anne, chided her mercilessly when she showed her the doll. "Throwing money away! Giv-ing an expensive doll like that to a five year old! It will be destroyed in no time!" But my grandma, for all her God-fearing insensitivity, had read me differently: as a child capable of valuing a beautiful doll. When I re-turned, summer after summer, with Patsy in peachy condition, Grandma Lizzie always found reason to take me next door. "Oh, Darlin', bring Patsy along," she'd say. "She'd probably like to visit Ray Anne too." I realize such visits were my grandmother's means of self-exoneration; but looking back, I also feel like she wanted to exonerate me. To show her neighbor that I could be trusted. Patsy will be fifty years old this Christ-mas. Perhaps I'll take her from the rocker in my bedroom and set her by the tree in honor of the single bond I felt with my maternal grand-mother. Her one vibrant act of faith was in me.

These are my grandmas, women I didn't really know and for whom I feel little more than compassion and a wispy kind of fondness. But because I called them Grandma, I find the name doesn't stick to my heart, regard-less of how many times I plaster it there thinking it might take the graft.

And then there's my children's grandma, my mother, Addie. She broke the G-mold beginning with her impressive debut in the waiting room the night Justin was born. Get this: my doctor, a dear, kind man in his sixties, a man who commented on how beautiful the night sky was when summoned to my side at 2 A.M., asked *while sewing me up,* how old my mother was. It seems he'd gone to the old-fashioned trouble of going to the waiting room to introduce himself before taking to his cot to "dream of babies" until the ordained moment arrived. He'd apparently been so taken with my mother that when summoned to delivery, he'd dropped by again to tell her he was "going to go get that baby for her." I knew why he wanted to know her age. She didn't look old enough to be anybody's grandmother. And evidently, from his delicate, suturing point-of-view, not old enough to be my mother either.

In my mind, my mother has been the perfect transgenerational grandmother. She was and remains nurturing and humorous, delighting in her five grandchildren while hardly ever mistaking their lives for her own. Regardless of whether she's lived in the same town with them or a full day's ride away, she's been involved with each one without compromising her sanity or her style.

Then there was my father. The ideal grandfather of boys might take them horseback riding. My father owned the horses. The ideal grandfather might teach his grandsons how to play baseball. My father built them an official-sized diamond on his ranch. (Taking off a corner of the barn when it got in the way.) An ideal grandfather might take those same boys to see their local baseball team play. My father took them to Yankee Stadium (twice) because the Yankees were their team. You get the picture. He was far from perfect, mind you, lapsing as he did sometimes into his old habits of impatience and control. But no one wondered how he felt about his grandkids, including the innocent upon whom he foisted their adorable pictures while my mother tamed her grimace into a smile.

And yet, he never wanted to be called Grandpa.

He coached Justin from his earliest days to call him "Bapa"; and even now, though he has been gone for several years, his grandchildren never call him anything else. Most of their lives, and until the day my mother took possession of his car, the frame on his license plate read, "World's

Greatest Bapa." As if he'd been elected king of some elitist club instead of a club invented by and for himself.

So in imitation of my clever genes, which did all those complicated calculations so many years ago, I'm striving for some pleasing blend of my parents when it comes to grandparenting: my mother's ability to be devoted without wearing her role like a bad muumuu, and my father's uncanny ability to steer clear of stereotypes—starting with crowning himself Bapa.

Soon after Nikki and Justin were married, when my mother first started dreaming of becoming a great-grandmother, she made an inadvertent error. "Just think," she said, "when Justin and Nikki have a baby, I'll be the mother of a grandmother." That's probably the moment I decided not to be called one even when I became one. I know, I know. You can dub yourself Gigi or Mimi or Zippity-do-ma and everyone on earth still knows exactly what that means: you're somebody's grandma.

Nevertheless, I decline the moniker.

January 14

I met my friend Lauren today for our annual post-Christmas birthday celebration. We both have late December birthdays, which is why a number of years ago, we started whipping out next year's virgin Hallmark pocket calendars to set a lunch date for January. We always go to the same place. Café California has been our spot since the inception of this celebration and the ritual always feels so lovely to me. "Ah, here we are again … let's order the wine … is this our sixth year? … what are you having? … how was your Christmas? … lunch looks beautiful … remember the time … this year let's take another trip … yes, we'll have dessert … shall we open the cards?" All leading up to the grand finale: the presents. Lauren shops exclusively at Nordstrom's—that is, unless she's recently been to New York City. I have an enviable under-bed stash of

Nordy's gold and silver gift boxes with elegant sliding bands around their middles. Another one today. She smiles surreptitiously as my annual act of band-sliding and lid-lifting ensues. Inside is a small, highly-padded, black leather photo album with red leather trim and tie.

"For baby pictures," she says. "I couldn't possibly get you anything that says 'Grandma's Brag Book'."

I feel the rise of emotion in my throat. Partly because it's the first tangible evidence of my changing status. Mostly because my friend knows me so well.

Second Trimester

Second-hand Futon Causes Psychological Setback

January 21

Off to Portland today. It will be my first time to see Nikki since the news. When I arrive at the house with Justin she's still at work. The pregnancy journal I sent is on the coffee table, but otherwise the living room is unchanged. But the back bedroom, which will be the baby's nursery, has undergone great alteration already. And not for the better. Sunny computer room has turned household slum. A stray piece of exercise equipment, an outcast from the little metal empire that makes its home in the garage, sits amidst cast-off items from the room's prior life: a lamp, a basket full of unarranged dried flowers, a square table holding an outdated printer. The gallery of family photos now drifts aimlessly across the wall, no longer anchored by the desk. The faces appear to be dutifully presiding over the chaos but otherwise uncommitted to life in this house.

"So look in the guest room," my son says with obvious pleasure. I look. What had been my little visitor's haven with a comfy, down-enhanced bed and a reading lamp within easy reach, is now a computer/guest room. Except that there is no bed. Instead the computer desk sits in cozy proximity to a metal futon that's been purchased from the neighbors. No down. No wall to lean against to read. And a computer for a roommate—almost a bedmate. "Oh, wow," I say, which is what I often say when my real thoughts are deemed inappropriate. "Getting things moved around already I see." He nods appreciatively. I unpack, telling myself that the cushion on the futon looks plenty thick and that I might as well break it in. If it weren't this visit, it would certainly be the next. I speak quietly to myself about the inevitability of change, but when I go to bed that night I make a discovery: the futon cushion is precious little protection from the intrusion of the underlying metal bar. And that's when I have a change of heart—and not the kind usually attributed to that phrase. Suddenly I mind being prematurely ousted from my comfy space and thrust into my not-yet-grandma quarters. I lie there trying to find my way around a metal rod while my grandchild floats in a water-bed forty times his or her size. Oh how I wish that my children, in their completely understandable state of restlessness, would have stuck with their battle of names and left my space alone.

January 22

Justin and I hit Fred Meyers today for one of those foam egg-crate things. It's appropriately the color of yolks and conveniently on sale. I feel elated paying the twenty-some dollars to insure a decent night's rest and a reduction of bed-envy toward my wholly innocent grandfetus. When Nikki gets home that night and sees my purchase, she informs me that there's a foam mattress in the overhead storage. Hmm. Evidently Justin didn't retain this bit of household minutiae, but no matter. I prefer my shiny egg-yolk crate to something that may have been on numerous camping trips with various unknown persons. However, when I peel the skin-tight wrapping off my purchase, there's this awful odor that could only be described as a blend of mold and skunk. I lay it out on the futon, trusting that it will air itself out by bedtime; but hours later, when I enter the room drowsy and hopeful, the smell hits me in the olfactory gut. I cover the offending foam with a blanket and then a sheet, but such measures are useless against the barrage of moldy skunk. So I bury my head in the pillow and assure myself that once asleep—*comfortably* asleep this time—the smell won't bother me. Regrettably, the struggle of mind over mattress doesn't end with losing consciousness. Every time I awake in the night, the skunk is nuzzling its stinky little head into my nostrils and by morning, I can't get the thing off the bed fast enough.

January 23

The worse-for-wear, dull green, but benign-smelling foam came down from the storage space this morning, and my pretty sun-colored mattress went back to Freddy's. Even the cashier scrunched up her nose in a show of sympathy when I passed it over the counter to her.

I pocketed the cash and left my bedding woes behind, ready for a far more appealing excursion. Though Nikki looks no different yet, her regular clothes are starting to chafe at the waist and we have decided to foray into the land of maternity wear. On the way to the mall, I tell her about my favorite maternity garb, speaking of it like a once-dear, nearly-forgotten ball gown. I recall vividly the day I found it, hanging on the sale rack in the middle of a small maternity shop. Sale or no, to me it was the most beautiful garment there, fulfilling as it did my longing for elegance in pregnancy and for a sense of style that transcended shape. The dress itself was simple: a black, brown, and white plaid tweed with an empire waist and three-quarter length sleeves. *But it came with a matching cape!* Perhaps it had found its way to the sale rack because people crossing that particular threshold thought it an oddity to be encaped, as if being rotund already didn't call for the added flair of plaid drapery. But I thought it a marvel of elegance, and bought it without trying it on.

Before entering the mall proper, Nikki and I duck into the Seaside Cafe. This is always the ritual: lunch first, then shopping. We take a booth in the bar so we don't have to wait, and settle in for a private chat.

Nikki's in this wonderfully dreamy state of her pregnancy. The morning sickness has abated, she's ready to shop for a new wardrobe, and at the moment she's wholly enamored with the prenatal devotion of my firstborn. I'm all ears. It's not that I take credit for Justin's exemplary behavior. It's just that I am so well acquainted with my shortcomings as a young mother, back when I knew myself not at all, that it helps to hear this praise for my son. It pours a warm, oily salve on places that are still healing in me, places that can still smart even though I know I did my best and could have done much worse.

"I told you about the stocking gifts he gave me, didn't I? They were just so thoughtful—lavender bath salts and peppermint foot cream—and all with little notes about taking care of myself. My Dad was so impressed with that."

"So sweet," I say.

"And he's just so involved, Mom. Wouldn't miss a doctor's appointment for anything. And he doesn't just come with me either; he asks questions and writes things down."

"I'm so glad, honey." But my words are nothing compared to what I feel.

The only thing that mars this idyllic moment is my attention to what she's eating. I'm playing Food Cop in my head and deserve the indigestion that might follow. Nikki understands how important nutrition is during pregnancy, and I understand she's making an effort to be more discerning. What I don't understand is *why*, after all these years of avid self-improvement, I'm still intent on making *her* choices *my* business. By now the human race has gone to excessive lengths to prove that such behavior bears an inverse relationship to desirable results, and a rather strong correlation to undesirable ones. So I take a deep breath and remind myself that when I was pregnant the first time, I ate with such unenlightened abandon that the woman now sitting across from me would have despaired for my unborn child. And almost thirty years later, here's said child, intelligent, productive, and winning his pregnant wife's heart all over again. *Shut up,* I tell myself. *Shut up and eat your portabella mushroom sandwich.*

Lunch finished, we step out into the flow of the marketplace. Our sites are narrowed today. We are on a mission. Nikki finds a couple of tops with clever labels: "Duet" and "Mum's the Word," but has less success with finding the business clothes she needs. She also buys new undies. I try to remember if I had special underwear when I was pregnant. Surely no ordinary underwear would have accommodated the shape I distinctly recall: of someone wearing a basketball under her dress to feign pregnancy. And yet I have no recollection of special, stretchy garments like the ones Nikki chooses. But then again, underwear isn't exactly the stuff of which great nostalgia is made. Lastly Nikki chooses a new nightgown and I seize it as my contribution to the cause. She responds to my gesture with such genuine appreciation that a sweet and still-surprising notion steals over me: I'm shopping with a daughter.

Naming Drama Evokes Shadow Side of Model Citizen

January 24

Justin and Nikki are heavy into baby negotiations. Currently, the choice of baby names is juxtaposed against the issue of gender-knowledge. To know or not to know. To let the sound-waves give you their best shot or wait for the thrill of a delivery room pronouncement. It seems that Justin is willing to trade his strong preference for the latter in order to gain some naming leverage. Nikki, on the other hand, is willing to allow Quincy as a male middle name in exchange for the option To Know.

"So what's your preference for finding out the gender?" their neighbor Jane asks me. "Oh, I'd prefer to be surprised," I say, hoping that

I don't appear to be siding according to bloodlines. Evidently not the answer Jane was seeking. "Really?" she says, her face a flag of disbelief. She'd evidently assumed that any prospective grandmother worth her genealogical salt would want the advantage of tipping the nursery décor in one pastel direction or the other.

"Sorry," I say reflexively, but even I can hear that this response is more polite than true.

I learned today there's another naming drama in the works. One that carries strong high-wind advisories for me to stay in and stay quiet. Nikki's parents have their own name of preference: "Sarah." No male counterpart, I notice. But after all, their experience with boys' names is that they just end up like carefully considered purchases that never make it out of the bag. As near as I can tell, however, the *preference* for this name goes beyond what the word, in all its nicety, implies. At least in Nikki's version, they're coming across as lobbyists for the one *true name.* She seems a bit faux-frustrated by it, but then wags her head and smiles affectionately, as if to say, "*Those* two." I try to join her in spirit, but don't seem to hit the same mark of generosity. "Remind them," I say as lightheartedly as I can, "that they had two chances to name girls and didn't choose Sarah either time."

The problem arises later when I'm left alone in the house for awhile. Whereas some people do their muttering in the cozy confines of their own minds—or at least have the wherewithal to do it *under* their breath—I have the misfortune to mutter aloud, and if you really must know, it isn't even muttering. I flat out talk to myself. And what I'm hearing myself say isn't all that charitable. I try to step back. I take a deep breath. I gently begin to question myself: why does this bother me so much? Is it because I don't care for the name Sarah myself, evoking as it does the memory of Sarah Sue Jenkins, who made third grade recess so utterly *un*recreational for me? Is it because I know the name isn't even *low* on Nikki's list? Or because they aren't even offering a token boy's name? Then I remember that Nikki said Justin liked the name Sarah, akin as it is to his own preferences for the old-fashioned ones of Rachel and Hannah. I seize this bit of comfort and try to fashion it into resolution, but like a blanket that's too small, its satisfaction is only momentary. And before I know it, the floor has fallen out of my self-inquiry and I am sitting again in a pile of my own judgmental do-do.

Now I'm really doomed because I know exactly what that means. It's my experience that when self-inquiry fails, it means I simply haven't gone deep enough. And having some sense of where *deep enough* is headed, I feel myself backing away. Maybe later.

January 25

Nikki and I went out to run some errands today, and in that convivial energy that successful errand-running can produce, I found myself offering to help her organize the house before the baby arrives. Now, ninety-eight per cent of the daughters-in-law of the world would be offended at such an offer—and rightly so, I might add. But Nikki frequently wages war with the clutter within their walls and, to her dismay, never triumphs for long. And even more frequently, she gives voice to her frustration—not the wan, wish-it-were-different brand of frustration, but the kind marked by great sighs, rolling of eyes, and a flurry of redoubled efforts. And to prove it is, in fact, the real thing, she embraces my offer like one who has been told the lab results were wrong and she's going to live after all. Of course I'm happy that she's happy and at the same time, I'm aware of doing myself a favor too. I've lately become paperback pals with the great guru of organization, Julie Morgenstern, and I'm thinking that together, Julie and I will be able to finagle an empty drawer or two in the guest room. Perhaps we will be able to clear ample space in the hall bath for the contents of a visiting cosmetic bag. Maybe we can even make getting a meal less of a tactical undertaking, thereby outwitting the person who designed the kitchen, it seems, without understanding the value of accessible storage. And perhaps, if Julie and I really hit it off, we can even make room for the onslaught of baby gear that will descend upon this household with plaid-and-checkered fervor.

Nikki's mother called her tonight and, in the course of the conversation, asked if I was being "politically correct" about the baby's name. Nikki had her usual air of amusement when she told me about it, and I tried to reflect her attitude with like good sportsmanship, but felt my defenses inflating with heliuministic speed. I was getting haughty with the *implication* of the question. Until I realized what I disliked about it.

It reminds me of that thing I'm not ready to talk to myself about yet.

Busy Doctor Thwarts Woman's Attempt to Evolve

January 27

Off to see the doctor with the kids this morning. Or rather, off in *hopes* of seeing the doctor, and more specifically, having him share his stethoscope with me. It is the heartbeat of my grandchild that prods me out of a warm futon, causes me to dress hastily, and then sit patiently without so much as one dark, hot, sip of liquid love. But alas, the waiting room proves to be my final destination. Nikki and Justin emerge apologetically from the inner sanctum, saying the appointment had been cut short because Dr. Duran had been called into delivery. I'd been hoping that the experience might make instinct rise from its lethargic coil, charmed by the primal music of my grandchild's beating heart. I'd fantasized that if I could return to California and tell my friends with genuine enthusiasm, "I got to hear the heartbeat!" that they might have more hope for me. Because while some of them relate to my untoward state, others are concerned. Not concerned like as if I had gallstones—more like as if I was *getting* stoned. And many days, I join them in their quasi-state of worry. I, too, am uneasy about the slow-stirring of anticipation, the sluggishness of my gra*maternal* instincts. After all, my maternal instincts kicked in just fine. I didn't have to hear my firstborn's heartbeat to feel pride and wonder—and when I did hear that tiny ticking, my feelings were so strong they coalesced into a first nickname: "Ticketey."

So this morning I left the doctor's office feeling a little deflated. And not just because I didn't get to finish that article on the dangers of breast implants. I return home tomorrow, not to my friends as much as to myself, with no progress to report.

February 1

I'm back and settled into what passes for routine in my life. Working out of my own home, the days are remarkably familiar without ever yielding to true routine. The best-laid plans can be quickly routed by a sick pet, an important phone call, or a dearth of clean underwear. Or a mood. Out in the world, one works despite the undulations of mood. At home, the boss can be too easily cajoled into making allowances. I have made progress over the years working in and around my moods, but Unresolved Emotion is still a show-stopper. Without apology or consideration for my agenda, Unresolved Emotion sends routine packing—as if my years in the mental health profession gives It tacit permission to barge in unannounced like a long-lost colleague.

So today, UE sits atop my work, legs crossed, head tossed back, daring me to push past its demands. It's useless. I'll get nowhere until I address the issue I left hanging in the balance back in Portland. I sigh, push back my chair and face the exasperating truth: my reaction to Ginny and Sam's name fixation is a cover-up for my own hidden desire for control. For all I know, they're half-in-jest about the whole Sarah campaign.

But me, I'm keeping serious dragons at bay in my comparatively tiny skull. I'm concerned about drug use in childbirth (Nikki loudly and adamantly wants as much as she can get as soon as she can get it). I'm uptight on the issue of breastfeeding (we haven't spoken on the subject recently, but in previous years she's made it clear that she doesn't plan to offer her services). Then there's the inevitable question of daycare (the bane of two hard-working parents). And I know for a fact there are more dragons lurking in the shadowy recesses where those were stowed. It's convenient to be annoyed with Ginny and Sam because they presume that naming this grandchild is their prerogative; but the truth is, I'm not without my own agendas. And now, like the uncongealed frosting on the crumbling cake, I'm judging myself for wanting control! I've worked so long and diligently on myself for this? Arrragh!! I shoo the cat off the bed and collapse on its cool calico surface. This is definitely one of those days when I'm less enthusiastic about being *more* conscious.

Later

I'm feeling better after going out to dinner with Sandi and digesting my woes over vegetable lasagna and a glass of House Red. When I'm in such a disheartened state, her quiet, listening presence makes me think of that quotation about the *wheat* and the chaff. She's the soul of that description: someone who sorts out one-from-the-other and then gently blows the chaff away. By dinner's end, the remaining wheat was obvious: as much as possible, I have to let go of needing things to be a certain way. I must reach out again for my life's credo of *Trusting the Process.* The *chaff*, of course, was imagining that I had any control to let go of. Of all things in this world, having children should thoroughly and soundly divest one of that particular notion. Yet here I am, seeing if by any chance, it might work where the next generation is concerned.

Tonight under the covers, I start to understand my resistance to becoming a grandmother. Maybe I'm reluctant to enter their enthusiastic ranks because I *get* something that many of them don't. Maybe they are in denial about the reality of the situation here: that a grandchild presents the scary proposition of scaling the heights of Mt. Caring without the drug of Supposed Control. Because sooner or later, no matter how hard you try to extend the illusion, it's going to become clear that you're not on the board of directors. At best, you'll occasionally have the ear of one of the co-chairs, but only then if you do so respectfully and infrequently.

And then I have this thought, suddenly turning over in bed to accommodate the shift of perspective. Is it possible that *I'm* the one who doesn't get something here, uninitiated as I am? Maybe there's something behind the secret sorority grins of these women, something that the ones high up in the order, the wisest of them, have come to know. Maybe the luminescent face of a child you didn't carry and don't intend to raise, plugs your soul into some unforeseeable grace. Maybe grandchildren are a chance to tap into a love that shuns even the *pretense* of control.

I don't know if I can pledge to this sorority, but at least I'm gaining on the truth. I'm wading into my real reservations about becoming a grandmother. And they don't have to do with money or Christmas or distance. They have to do with me. They have to do with letting go yet again. They have to do with applying everything I've learned to a *situation* I know nothing about. They have to do with putting my beliefs to a new test. Beliefs of trusting the processes of the soul, of trusting Spirit and inner guidance, of trusting whatever life brings as a potential means to greater wholeness. Of trusting all these—even with a grandchild.

Customer Sees Sex in a Pillow

February 6

I was in a store called Beautiful Beds today looking for some new throw pillows. Doesn't the number of decorative pillows they put on those beds just slay you? *Only in model homes and linen stores,* I think to myself. In real life, you'd have to schedule time in your planner for dressing and undressing the bed. They have a great selection of pillows here though—most of them stacked on free-standing shelves. Not one to miss anything when on a search, I bend over, surveying the bottom row, then gradually raise myself, flamingo-style, to eye the top row. I then dip back down and begin again. On my third round, no doubt embarrassing flamingos everywhere, a little fake needlepoint pillow hanging from the vertical bar crosses my vision. "It's a Boy!" it exclaims, and my body utters, "Oh!" before my mind has a chance to show up and start bossing me around. But even then it feels like a bona fide message, the kind that comes when all you're really after is pillows, not prophecy. Because I really don't have an investment in this outcome. But now that this little Dacron-filled seed has been planted, I realize I'm smiling. I have my own secret about this babe who would fit in the palm of my hand right now. I know something no one else knows yet—or at least I think I do, which for the moment, is enough. I leave the store with no new pillows and a cheesy grin.

It's a boy.

February 14

My firstborn outdid himself today. Instead of sending roses to Nikki's workplace for Valentine's, he sent a custom-ordered, pregnant mama bear with roses in one hand and a heart in the other. She's wearing a maternity top that says, "Baby on Board." I'm privy to all this because Nikki called me on her way home sounding like a high-schooler whose boyfriend just gave her his class ring. (I know that description dates me, but so would "going steady" or the easily misconstrued "getting pinned.") I'm happy for her of course, but in a funny way, I'm happier for him. In the last few years, he seems to have developed a skill that eludes many men their whole lives: the talent for spousal gift-giving. I'm feeling confident that he won't suffer under the curse of lukewarm receptions, store-bought returns, or tucked-away rejects. Last Christmas he surprised Nikki with tickets to see the Trans-Siberian Orchestra—without knowing she'd heard them on the radio and wished they could go. For her birthday, he created an evening in the city: dinner out and good seats at the *Phantom of the Opera*.

It's funny how the advent of Justin's first child is making me see Justin himself differently. It's so hard to keep seeing your children when they're growing up, fraught as they are, as you are, with the stuff of everyday living. I still remember what it was like to see the boys again when I'd been away for a couple of days. Upon return, I was wearing new glasses, seeing them in sharp and breathtaking focus, instead of through the blurred lens of mommyhood. When Nikki called me with her news today, I saw Justin again in flashback: the hospital newborn, swimming in a blue bunting that I'd thought would fit him just right; the squirrelly grade-schooler with unruly hair and a tooth-gappy grin; the handsome, beaming high school graduate. After we hung up, I went back to my bedroom and pulled out his pictures: Justin at one, at two, at four, and saw once more how outrageously beautiful he was.

"My God," I whisper aloud, "did I *see* you?"

Not like I'm seeing you now.

I hold a picture of his tow-headed smile to my heart. Maybe a grandparent gets to have 20/20 vision in present tense.

February 20

Last night I dreamed that the baby is a boy. And I'm encouraged because it seems that at least unconsciously, the grandma self seems to be taking hold, as this little guy was extremely precocious. Isn't that what most grandmothers say as they gaze at their off-offspring's photo even after you've stopped looking? "He's extremely precocious." But to redirect your attention to my point: it was clearly a boy.

My mind showed up again, muttering of ego reinforcement and past dream debacles.

"You often dream of precocious babies," it says cynically. "All those walking, talking newborns you have yet to make sense of."

"But none of those were *grandsons*," I counter. "In fact, most of them were girls."

I usually try to keep these left-to-right brain arguments from proliferating into full-blown dialogues. If they go on too long, the hard-wired side tends to get the upper hand. Better to make my case succinctly and move on. So in the interest of that, I call my mother and tell her my dream.

"Honey," she says, after hearing it, "remember the dream I had a couple of years ago? Justin was walking down a country road toward me, holding the hand of an adorable little boy in short pants. It was so vivid that I remember telling you it felt like a premonition."

I do remember. And I also remember thinking that the dream was symbolic of her longing for a great-grandchild, and not necessarily prophetic. Of course my conclusion was no doubt muddied by the fact that hers was a longing I didn't share.

I still can't say I share that longing. But I can say this: my left brain was remarkably mum when I hung up the phone.

February 21

Nikki's nonchalant references to the baby as "her" and "she" are sounding strange to me now. And, meanwhile, her parents have closed the chromosomal gap by announcing that Nikki and Justin are free to name the baby whatever they want, but they're calling her Sarah. Now I *know* they're kidding. It does feel odd to be living in my alternate reality however—trusting messages from fake needlepoint pillows and trans-generational dreaming. But, as you probably notice, I'm not yet trusting them enough to counter the going consensus aloud.

Even in light of this assumed foreknowledge, I would still opt for a day-of-birth revelation. I'm partial to the notion of mounting suspense, bursting double doors, and a breathless proclamation from a man who's quaking with wonder. However, our two secret camps will be breaking up soon. Nikki and Justin have successfully completed their negotiations. Early knowledge of baby gender has been officially exchanged for certain naming rights. So it will be the stealthy eye of the ultra-sound that sees and tells all.

February 24

Between swallows of a Starbuck's Americano today, I tell Margaret about my gender-bending experiences. When I get as far as my mother's dream, she inadvertently exclaims, "Oh boy!" and we both laugh in merry, twinkling recognition. I leave our time together with that little, yellow two-piece suit on my mind, the one preserved by some far- away decision and double plastic bags. Suddenly, it morphs into an official shower gift, something special to hand down the line. And once I picture a baby boy inside it, I imagine having my very own *deja vu* with this child—a quick, glancing kiss with the past, a shimmering moment on the other side of the looking glass. For even the thought of holding a baby boy, fresh from womb and Spirit, brings Justin's newborn face so close to mine that I can hear him breathing. I have to admit that it's a thought that simultaneously frightens and thrills me. I'm scared that such a likeness might overwhelm me with the longing to do it all over, with the pulsing regret of all my young-mother flaws, and that such aching might crowd out elation. But when I turn that fear over, another hallowed thought greets me: this little boy will only know the person I've become—the far-from-perfect, but much more present, whole, and happy me.

It occurs to me that if I'm feeling *scared* and *thrilled*, I've crossed a threshold. No longer looking to generations fore and aft to compensate for my lack of emotion. It seems the grandma genes are stirring in their nest.

February 27

I've made a mental commitment to sign up for Baby CPR. No one who knows me would expect such a thing, and few would believe it unless repeated thrice with a straight face. Unfortunately, it's the kind of thing I'm more likely to think about than do. Hence the commitment. Here's the thing: on the one hand, I have absolutely no personal history to support the idea that I would, under any circumstances, be lucid or skilled enough to do the right thing in case of an emergency. And that part of me can think of several other ways to spend forty bucks and the better part of a Saturday. On the other hand, if I don't have a *clue* about what to do other than scream for help—which may only attract other clueless people—there's no chance at all of grace under pressure. It's the thought of being at the mercy of my own complete and utter ignorance that I can't abide.

Technology Faces Off With Ancient Art of Intuition

March 1

Tomorrow is the ultra sound. Since I've already conducted my own informal survey and am fairly confident of its results, I'm feeling pretty mellow. It's like waiting to get your official grades in the mail when you've aced most of your tests—not much in the way of suspense. On the other hand, it's possible that I'm just too smug for my own good.

I've asked Justin to call me with the news. Nikki is usually the first-line spokesperson for both of them, but this is something I want to hear from him. It may not be the flap of double doors and a mile of irrepressible grin; but still, it will be his dear, familiar voice in my waiting ear.

March 2

The old gut isn't waffling this morning. Still a boy. Besides, I figure that this early in a pregnancy, ultra-strong intuition may have just as much accuracy as ultra-sound.

Justin calls early this afternoon and I can tell by the tone of his *hi mom* that he doesn't know anything yet. It seems the doctor's equipment was on the fritz, refusing to offer cooperation sufficient to the task. So another ultra-sound is scheduled at the hospital in a couple of days.

I'm sticking to my story till technology gets its act together.

March 4

Today's the hospital ultra-sound and for some reason, I'm not as calm as the first time around. And tell me this: why is it that practically everyone you know decides to call when you're waiting for the Big Ring? I've explained to my body that I'm 92.8 per cent sure *it's* a boy, yet every time the phone rings, my heart revs up like a hot-rod with something to prove, reminding me of all those yesteryears of waiting for *the boy* to call. So now I'm waiting for *my* boy to call and tell me it's a boy. Anyway, I go through *that* whole thing half-a-dozen times this morning before I hear the voice my heart was holding out for.

"Hi, Mom," he says in that endearing, lyrical way of his. Today his voice is round, holding something precious. "It's a boy."

"Just what I thought, honey!" I say, without stopping to elaborate. "Are you happy?"

"Yeah, I really am!"

"And Nikki?"

"She's okay with it. We talked about it afterward and she didn't seem disappointed at all."

"And it's for sure?"

"They used two different machines and both of them gave the same outcome."

"I didn't want to tell you until now, Just, but I had a dream that it was a boy."

"Really? So did Nik."

"She *did?*"

"Yeah, a few weeks ago. I'm sure she'll tell you about it when she calls."

"Well, thanks for calling, honey. Congratulations."

"Thanks, Mom. I love you."

"Oh, I love you, too—so much."

Later today I'll get all the intricate details from Nikki. But for the moment, I savor what I got from my son: the audible smile in his voice, the sweetness that has always been a part of him, the sacredness of this moment. Justin's calls are typically more about exchanging information than exchanges of heart, and yet, his heart comes through. I sit down and feel his presence, as if he is sitting here with me in the stillness.

My boy is having a boy.

A few hours later

Nikki calls on her lunch hour. No hint of disappointment transmits itself across the wires.

"Mom," she says immediately, "I knew it was a boy."

"Justin said you had a dream."

"I did. A couple of weeks ago. And when I woke up, Justin was standing in the doorway and I said, "Oh, Just, it's a boy." He played it down and I was willing to go along because I've had my heart set on a girl, but the feeling never left me. And the closer we got to the ultrasound, the more sure I was."

"Guess what? I had a dream it was a boy too."

"You failed to mention that," she says with mock disapproval.

"I didn't want you to think I was rooting for a boy, consciously or unconsciously. I'll tell you about it later, but give me more scoop. Justin says the results were pretty definitive."

"Not to begin with, which is why they switched to another machine. The second one left little doubt—though my Mom's still leaving room for error. She had a friend whose results were wrong several years ago so she's still holding out for a granddaughter."

"Do *you* have any doubt?"

"Uh, no. We had views from three angles, Mom. It's a boy."

"And your Dad?"

"I just finished talking to him. He's thrilled and making plans." She chuckles to herself. "And of course, I think we've probably heard the last of Sarah."

"There you go! The baby's not even here yet and he's already a skillful problem solver."

"Oh! And did Just tell you? We have a beautiful profile of his face!"

After we hang up, I sit and stare into space. Everything I have to do seems infinitely small and just outside my reach. *He has a profile,* I keep thinking. And then I have to back up. *No wait—he has a face!* I try to envision what the profile of a four-month-old-fetus might look like. But curiously, it's like trying to imagine growing breasts when I was ten or picture leaving for college when I was still in junior high. I have absolutely no reference for something so extraordinary. No way to make such a wild and wondrous possibility my own.

March 5

Nikki just amazes me sometimes. Since the beginning of our relationship, her dreams have been a source of astonishment to me. For example, in one dream she went back and lived certain parts of her life over, all the while remembering the nature and truth of her waking life, and continually comparing the two realities. So this latest dream experience isn't all that surprising given her nocturnal history. What's more surprising is that she listened to it—even when it wasn't the answer she was looking for. And now, perhaps she's surprised herself: not just with acceptance, but with the agility and speed of it. "The disappointment was so fleeting, Mom," she'd told me just hours after getting the news. "By the time I left the doctor's office I was thinking, *Okay then, I'm going to be the mother of a son!* And you know, it felt just right.

"I've always loved being the mother of sons," I'd say in truthful response.

"And now you have me for a daughter!"

"My *only* daughter as you always remind me."

"Yeah, and remember, let's keep it that way."

Nikki is a Leo, and like most Leos, she yearns to be the exclusive member of at least one club.

March 12

A new and more serious level of baby naming has broken out in the suburbs of Portland. Lauren, of course, has been discarded along with Sarah, Hannah, and Rachel. Nikki was quick to re-establish her male favorite, however: Ryan. Unlike the name Lauren, it's a name she's fancied since high school years. Now, I have no objections to the name Ryan; in fact, I even have some fond associations with it. But I don't like it with Bowes. Too soft. Too bland. Too passive. Bowes is a name that needs a punch out in front of it. Gimme a K! gimme a J! a G or a D! Even a hard C.

I do like Dillon, one of Justin's long-running favorites, but now that sound-wave results have been traded for the middle name of Quincy, Dillon is out. This baby's astute and considerate parents are taking no chances on having their firstborn dubbed "DQ." So I find myself running lots of possibilities along with the shower water each morning, but I don't really come up with anything that inspires me. It's just as well. I'm trying to stay out of having a stake in the matter—other than my private little objections to the gelatinous sound of Ryan Bowes.

March 15

Today my time in the steam was dedicated to my own naming. In the beginning it was enough to definitively reject the title of Grandma, to clear the decks and declare myself open to untold possibilities. But lately, there's this big, smudgy spot in my mind where the word Grandma used to be, and I'm feeling compelled to fill it in.

I meet my friend, Lauren, this morning at our designated mid-way Starbucks for our designated drink, the classic and consistently hot Americano. So much more than a mere cup of coffee. It was Lauren who introduced me to it on a trip to L.A. years ago when the two of us recouped a bit of our repressed adolescence by playing groupies to Gavin's band. So every cup comes with the added perk of fondness by association.

Settled on the little corner platform that is prime real estate at this particular Starbucks, scone between us, I present my need for a name.

"Why the rush?" she asks. "He's not going to call you anything for awhile."

"I know, but *other people* need to call me something *to* him once he's born. You know, like 'Go see Nana' and 'Mimi's here!' etc. Besides, if I don't start coaching them soon, the great default setting of the ages will take over."

"Oh, he'll probably come up with his own name anyway. That's the job of a firstborn."

"But I have to give him something to work with. Help me come up with the raw material here."

She rolls her eyes at me, and I think resists an urge to shake her head.

"Oh what do you know?" I respond, laughing. "You're not a grandma. Not even a pregnant one."

On the way home I do get this burst of inspiration. Not as in original inspiration, mind you. More along the line of *appropriated* inspiration. Gavin's former girlfriend and honorary family member, Jenny, had a talent for original, affectionate naming. She called Brad, "Bradley-Dadley." She called me "Mommadel." "Mommadel," I say aloud as I lean into the long curves along Fair Oaks Boulevard, testing this new use of a beloved endearment. It works—soft, unique, and already familiar to the family. It also has a charming, faintly Southern ring that conjures up long afternoons of sipping iced tea while sitting on a wide, wrap-around porch—a touch of genteel matriarchy. Or have I just been reading too much Ann Rivers Siddons lately?

Landscaper Fertilizes Old Anxieties

March 18

Our friend Trina is in the process of landscaping our front yard. Last year she gave birth to her sixth child, a little girl who rides papoose while her mother creates sensuous burms and pathways in the space formerly held hostage by ivy. I offer her lunch today and over toasted cheese sandwiches tell her Nikki and Justin are expecting a boy. She begins to ask me some questions about Nikki's plans for childbirth, and gently cautions me about the trend of inducing labor. "It's so common these days," she says. "But what first mothers don't understand is that with inducement, there's no build-up of pain. You go right into hard labor. And the sudden onset of intense pain often sets off a chain of events that results in a higher percentage of cesareans."

Her warning, as sensitive and informed as it is, rekindles the embers of control. The phone is suddenly a giant magnet pulling me toward it, commanding me to warn Nikki of the dark side of elective inducement. It is a particularly strong pull because Nikki is not, by nature or her own admission, a patient person. I could see her on the due date—or even before—saying, "Okay, that's enough! Let's get on with it!" On the other hand, her threshold for pain is renowned. And not because it's high. After Trina returns to the yard, I eye the phone earnestly, but turn away. There's no real rush except the one in my gut.

March 19

Yesterday's conversation about inducement has lit up my internal switchboard. Calls are coming in from all over the emotional map: arguments for natural childbirth versus (what's the term here?) *un*natural childbirth? birth by drugs? And those calls are intermingled with impassioned pleas in favor of breastfeeding versus bottle feeding. This inner debate gets completely out of control before I think to ask myself the obvious question: *What* am I getting so worked up for? Step back and take a look here, my dear woman. Is this something like: "Well, I'm still not convinced I'm ready for a grandchild, but since the two of you insist on having one, do you mind if I call the shots?"

It's definitely time to take a deep breath and do a bit of recollecting: I partook of drugs at childbirth; the fact that they were minimal had more to do with being built-to-have-babies than with great endurance. If a certain pelvic structure hadn't been my lot, I no doubt would have gladly traded pain for greater comfort, ignorant as I was about the effect of drugs on the unborn. And as for breast feeding, yes, I did it and I'm glad—especially now that I know something about it. Yet I don't recall even making the decision. My doctor probably endorsed it. I can tell you for a fact, it wasn't because I did the research. So, a deep breath and recollecting have done their job. Now I know why I'm so worked up. What's upsetting me is this: I know more *now* than I did *then* about matters that no longer pertain to me. Kind of like knowledge with a personal expiration date. My only hope, then, is getting *someone* else to use information that is no longer applicable to me. Poor Nikki. It seems there are dues to be paid for being the single member of the "Only Daughter Club."

March 20

I had a revelation today. I tried it out on Sandi as soon as she got home from work. "Hey," I say, following her around the house while she sifts through the junk mail and pets the cats. "I realized something today."

"Uh huh," she says with neither excitement nor disinterest. My revelations are frequently part of her transition from the work world to domestic life.

"You know how I was so troubled about all the birth stuff a couple of days ago and wondered how much to say to Nikki?"

"Un huh."

"I realized that I can accept whatever she decides as long as she considers the options. Well, maybe with the exception of inducing labor—that would require more time in the acceptance chamber."

"Tell her that then. About considering the options, I mean."

"Leave out the part about more time in the acceptance chamber?"

"At least for now."

Sandi, of course, knows why the inducement thing is a special hook for me, and it's not what you're thinking. I wasn't induced myself, pushed out of the womb before my time. O Contraire! Two nurses held me back waiting for the doctor to arrive. No, my grievance with inducing labor is professional. I make my living as an astrologer. Not the predictive good year/bad year kind, but rather the kind who quotes Carl Jung: "Whatever is born in a moment of time bears the qualities of that moment." I believe that in some mysterious way, the soul comes forth at a moment that reflects its own calling, its own talents and challenges. Even if you totally eschew astrology, I'm sure you can see that unnecessarily inducing a child's birth wouldn't make such a person smile. Necessary intervention is a different matter, but under normal circumstances I'm all for waiting on the soul's timing. It's not that pat exactly. Nothing of the soul ever is. There are reasons, I believe, for everything, including having others jump start your entrance into the world. It's just that such a scenario would be hard for me to accept.

Of course, I'm not the one who will be nine months pregnant in July either.

Career Woman Held Hostage By Domestic Engineer

March 21

This is fascinating. I have a front row seat to the Hormonal Power and Light Show. A little over five months into her pregnancy, Nikki, whose career success has turned heads and overturned policy—that same Nikki—wants to be home. *Now.* "My heart just isn't in it the way it used to be," she tells me repeatedly. "I love the company I work for and I'm feeling good, but I just want to be home."

"So it's already starting to feel different to you now," I say in my very best non-directional Carl Rogers tone. But inwardly I'm reeling. Rolling before my eyes is a vision of Amazon Nikki—stuffed into a closet, limbs flailing against the door while Domestic Nikki slips a key into the pocket of her checkered apron, smirking as she walks away.

"And the baby isn't even here yet! How will I feel when that happens?! Last night I tried to get Justin to go get a second job," she says with a hint of levity, "but he won't do it."

"Did you ever think you would feel this way, Nik?"

"Never, Mom," she says solemnly.

I hang up the phone feeling strangely moved. My son married an ambitious, independent young woman who's never vacillated about wanting a career *and* children. I've always thought she was right about that, and yet five months into the carrying of her first child, something ancient is pulling on the flap of her suit jacket—imploring her to follow her body's march toward utter renovation, calling her to reconfigure her life around an invisible beating heart.

"Oh dear God," I say to myself, "she's already fallen in love."

March 23

After sitting with my Mommadel inspiration for several days, I shared it tonight with Justin and Nikki, consecutively. He seems pleased enough. She is quiet. "Hmm. I'll have to think about that," she finally says. I've known Nikki long enough to know what such a response means: she doesn't like the name, but is choosing to be diplomatic. I let it go, hoping the idea will grow on her.

March 24

I'm spending an inordinate amount of time these days stalking the aisles of Circuit City where Good Guys can get their Best Buy. I've hit them all in search of a shower gift for my grandboy. These are not the kind of places I'd envisioned shopping for a baby, but I'm finding pleasure in doing the unexpected, in coming at this new self in my own way. And when it comes to gifts, for the born or unborn, my way has always been a strange concoction of intuition, inspiration, and a talent for turning the off-handed comment into an entry on my gift list. Since Unnamed Baby Boy has given me no hints, handed or off-handed, I'm relying solely on intuitive sources, which strongly suggest a boom box. Not some big, blaring, black thing—oh, no. Something small, pastel, and of decent quality, one with both tape deck and CD player. (Sometimes intuition is in a mood to be particular.) This box will be accompanied by a collection of CDs. Lullabies to start: soft, ephemeral, floating melodies to soothe and enchant the newborn. Later we'll progress to nursery rhyme fare, and then to silly singalongs, but for now, all things gentle.

In the meanwhile, the perfect boom box eludes me.

March 25

The boom box inspiration is really Part Three of a larger inspiration schema: the trans-generational gift. Something from my childhood, something from Justin's childhood, and something from the baby's own generation. So today my attention shifts to the other shower offerings. I pull Justin's little yellow suit out from under its layers of protective plastic, planning to give it a gentle wash. On closer inspection, however, I realize why it's in such good condition: it was never worn. The size must not have matched the season, the short pants too cold even for a California winter. It looks new, except for being dated. I don't recall seeing Scottie Dogs on infant wear lately, though I can't quite say what has replaced them. Boxers? Schnauzers? I sit on my bed grimacing at the thought of giving my grandchild an unwashed thirty-year-old garment, but I know that washing will remove its pristine finish and make it look *exactly* like what it is. Perhaps Nikki will want to use it as nursery décor. And if she decides to have him wear it, gently wash it I will.

The gift from my childhood has traveled with me down through the decades, surviving my occasional household purgings in the honorable efforts of stuff-reduction. It was mine as a very young child: a set of four small, pastel hardback books, aged, but in excellent condition. Winnie-the-Pooh. I imagine reading to my grandson from "Now We Are Seven" or "House at Pooh Corner," and a wave of feeling crashes on some inner shore, nostalgic and tidal. My mother read these books to me. I read them to my sons. And soon … the tears smart and startle … soon Christopher Robin will be banging Pooh's head on the stairs once again—only this time it will not only be my book and my voice, but the weight of my grandchild, warm and trusting against me.

March 26

Nikki's hormonal shift has gone seismic. With little notice, she took time off from work, telling her boss it would be at least a week, maybe two. "But I don't know if I'll be ready even then, Mom," she confides. "I just want to be home." Her last words come out like a whimper, the plea of a small child who has been dragged about the adult world too long and is rapidly caving in on herself.

"What a good choice, honey," I say sincerely, while at the same time quelling a question from some other quarter of my brain: can you afford it? I nix the query. She doesn't need the question and I don't need the answer.

"I can't explain it," she says, her voice crackly with tears. "I just can't focus on work. I know I still care about my job, but …"

"You don't *feel* like you care right now."

"I *don't*. I feel bad giving Carolyn such short notice—even though she was great about it. But I just can't be there right now."

"You're doing the right thing, Nik. You're listening to yourself, and this break is probably what's going to get you through the months ahead."

"I hope so."

By the time we hang up, I'm thinking about her boss, Carolyn. She's Nikki's Mother-Mentor in the world of business. They're close and Nikki is one of her top producers. I give her credit for supporting Nikki's leave of absence. She has to be wondering if this dash for the ancient cave is a herald of things to come. I wonder too, but unlike her, I don't have big numbers riding on it. I stop and silently bless this woman I've never met. Evidently out in the hard-driving world of business, there are still those who see beyond the numbers that fuel their days.

March 28

Nikki has more time to think now. Subsequently, I got the official name veto today. I was more disappointed than surprised, having inwardly made Mommadel my own.

"It's too much like Mama, and *I'm* the Mama," she told me after gently broaching the subject.

"But you call your grandma 'Grandmama'" I respond, in equally gentle protest.

"But it starts with 'grand,' and besides, that's what most grandmas are called in the South.

Ah, the South! Just what I was subconsciously trying to evoke.

"It's okay, Nik. I understand."

"I'm sorry," she says. "I know you love that name 'cause Jenny Lou gave it to you."

"I do, but I'll find another. It'll be fine."

Of course, I think to myself as I hang up. *Of course no new mommy wants her husband's mother, however loved, to have the first two syllables* of her own name. Still, I feel sad and a little rejected. I sigh and momentarily consider simply going by Maridel and letting Baby make his own name of it. Maybe it would come out something cute like "Mardie" or "Adel."

But then again, it could emerge as "Mudel" or "Airdale." Or worse.

Oh yes, these are the consequences of openly resisting tradition.

March 29

Sandi and I pay a visit to Target tonight. She wants one of those Mama Teddy bears with a heartbeat for Nikki and Justin. They look like regular Teddies, but when you turn the dial, a whooshing heartbeat emanates from furry pores. And the heartbeat is the real thing too. Recorded from inside the womb, it replicates what baby has been hearing all those months once the womb has closed up shop. En route to Babyland, I pay my habitual visit to the electronic department. Leave it to Sandi to spot a boom box display I hadn't seen at the end of an aisle. It's the perfect specimen: small, round, pearly-blue and silver, capable of playing both tapes and CDs.

"And why does it need to play both again?" she asked once we'd committed it to the cart.

"Just to have the option. Plus lots of children's books come with tapes."

Actually, there's another reason I want the boom box to have a cassette player, but I'm not quite ready to confess why. Last month when I reorganized all the tapes and CDs, I had this idea. I could make one of those mixed tapes for the Baby: Billy Joel's lullaby, *Good Night, My Angel* from his River of Dreams album; Bill Wither's rendition of *Lean on Me*; Whitney's version of *Jesus Loves Me* from the soundtrack of The Bodyguard. Plus other songs that are no doubt hiding out in the plastic confines of my collection.

I could tell Sandi, of course, but somehow I'm a little embarrassed. It seems so personal, so sentimental, so like what you do when you're in love. In fact, I've done it in the past for that very reason, choosing with care every selection as well as the intimate flow of the sequence. Doing it for a baby wouldn't feel like that, I'm sure. I don't fancy myself to be in love, though I have noticed over the years that whether in gravity or relationship, leaning often leads to the act of falling.

And leaning I am. Definitely leaning I am.

April 3

I'm packing for my Organizing-Guru-Meets-Baby-Shower trip to Portland. Quite the scene. First of all, I'm flying, and therefore have to abide by the reasonable, yet severely limiting guidelines of modern aviation. Secondly, organizing aspirations aside, here's a fact: layettes are considerably easier to pack than boom boxes. I never think of these earthy matters under the spell of inspiration—not that thinking of them would stop me, you understand. Then, there are the requirements of my Julie Morgenstern imitation. Here in my hometown, I know exactly where to get good and affordable essentials: wire shelves of different lengths and levels; colored plastic bins of varying sizes, some that stack; and a few serviceable baskets. And, of course, my copy of *Organizing From the Inside Out*. So join me in calling myself crazy, but a box of bins and shelves are going with me. Well, not *with* me exactly. My unsightly, cut-to-size, taped together box will be stowed in the belly of the plane. Only Julie will hop on board with me. I'd rather be seen with her anyway.

Oregon Couple Wins "Name That Baby!" Contest

April 5

Justin picks me up at the Portland airport and quickly heaves my suitcase and klutzy box into the covered bed of his truck. Surprise, it's raining. I can't tell by the look on his face whether he's amused or inwardly eye-rolling. "It's just shelves and baskets," I say, trying to reassure him that his casual style of living isn't about to be regimented against his will. Or maybe it is and I want to reassure him anyway.

We go to our favorite place for lunch, a place I wanted to eat based on the name alone: "John Barleycorn's." It's one of many establishments owned by the McMenamin brothers in Portland and beyond. This one is a pubby, church bench, microbrewery kind of place that not only has great food (we always succumb to the fish tacos), but also the advantage of being just a stone's throw from Trader Joe's, where I routinely do my home-away-from-home shopping. While waiting for our Sea-Mex feast, we talk about baby furniture, Nikki's continuing hiatus and inevitably, baby names. I express my Ryan Bowes objection—not much of a risk since Justin isn't a Ryan fan. "I've never liked it that much, really," he says. "It's too common." I smile, remembering that this is a child who not only started life with an unusual name himself, but one who had a Waldorf education. Waldorf, as you might suspect by its own name, is a place where names like Bronwein, Govind and Uma are the order of the day, rather than provocation for shameless teasing.

"Believe it or not, Justin was an unusual name when Dad and I chose it. Everyone thought it was so novel. We only came across one person who knew of a Justin, and it was his own grandfather. But a few years later, no soccer team was complete without its requisite Justin. How does that happen?"

"I don't know exactly, but I'll show you the list I printed off the Internet. It has the top one hundred names of the last few years. They do go in cycles."

"I can understand names going in cycles when there's a list, and people content to chose something because it's popular. But we didn't have a PC or a list, and we intentionally set out to choose a name that was unusual."

"I guess you and Dad just started a trend, then," he says with his sly signature smile.

I smile in return. "Well, I wouldn't change it anyway. You make a great Justin."

I don't talk astrology with my son much. Partly because I don't like it when the astrologically-inclined foist their secret language on the unsuspecting, turning every dialogue into an astrologue. And partly because, while he seems accepting of my profession, he doesn't seek out my astrological counsel. And I take the cue. But hearing myself say, *You make a great Justin,* I take a starry moment for myself. I knew nothing about astrology when he was born, and yet we named this child, born under the sign of Libra, Justin, meaning "Just," or "One of Justice." The Libran glyph is the scales, the classic symbol of justice, and my son has made his professional home in the judicial system, to which so many Librans are drawn. It occurs to me now that it was really his angels who named him. We were just lucid enough to be listening.

As our taco platters are served, I eye my son adoringly and realize what I want for Nikki and for him—not just a name they agree on, but a name that will feel perfect thirty years later over a rainy day lunch. I wish them a name that is beloved to them, a name that becomes more so with every milestone of their son's life. A name that suits him so well they don't remember there was ever a list.

After lunch we head over to Trader Joe's. If you haven't ever been to a TJ's, I can't help you. No matter how ardently I describe it, it's going to come off sounding like a grocery store. Of course, that's what it is fundamentally, but it so transcends the grocery store vibe that I long ago stopped thinking of it as one. It's this cordial, eclectic, creative place where shopping for food is more of an adventure than a task. I have no official research with double-blind designs and statistically significant results, but I swear to you that people are downright pleased to come see Joe. My friend Stephanie drives about forty miles round trip to do business with him, and when I remarked on her outlay of time and energy, she smiled like a woman in love and said, "Believe me, it's no hardship."

At TJ's, people confer in the aisles like old neighbors, exchanging tips on the goods. And the goods themselves are endlessly fascinating, of excellent quality and yet, reasonably priced. The staff is good-humored in a casual, human way, aided in attitude by their Hawaiian shirts. The food demos are stylish and yummy. And with every visit, you find new temptations that make you want to take the shortcut home: dark chocolate pistachio-covered toffee, cranberry-cinnamon goat cheese, or black bean jalapeno chips. And like my friend Sharyn says, where else could you get a bag of frozen red, yellow, and green peppers called *Mélange a Trois?*

Justin likes Joe's too. He tosses a few treasures into the cart with my staples of yogurt cheese, Woven Wheat Wafers, Barbara's Oat Squares, a couple of bottles of Charles Shaw Cabernet, and a bar of Joe's own 72 per cent dark chocolate. We pick up some supplies for the household as well, and Justin snatches a cone of fresh flowers for Nikki at the check stand.

When Nikki comes through the door a few hours later, fresh from the hairdresser, my breath catches in my throat. Someone in me—evidently someone who hasn't been keeping up—inwardly exclaims, "She is pregnant!" For the first time, it's obvious. We stand in the middle of the floor and hug each other tightly, and between us I can feel her belly pressing into mine. "What do you think?" she asks as she steps back. "I definitely think you're pregnant," I say. "And wearing it well. You look great."

"Oh!" she says suddenly, and I half-expect her to double over and grab a chair, but instead she whirls away from me and pulls something off the fridge.

"I'm sorry we didn't get this copied for you, but here he is!"

The profile of the baby's face is suddenly whisked close to mine, with nary a moment to pray I'll be able to recognize it.

"See?" she says, as Justin joins us. The three of us stand together, hovering on the brink of kitchen and wonder as I take the black-and-white photo in my hand.

"Wait, just give me a second," I say.

"Here's the forehead," she prompts, unable to hold back. And all of a sudden, a face arises from the page—a face in perfect profile.

"Oh my God," I say as my hand flies to my mouth. And I mean it. This isn't just a profile on a page. It's a person.

"Very few people get an image like this," they're saying in the background. "The tech just happened across it and took it for us."

I can barely hear them. I'm looking at the eye, the outline of the ear and the jaw, but I'm seeing something more. He has a look. He looks old and wise to me, as if he's gazing down a long, long road with deep understanding. My mind flashes on the pictures I've seen of very young children chosen as leaders of a spiritual lineage. They all have a certain countenance of knowing and peace. It's the look I hold in my hand.

"He's beautiful," I breathe, reluctant to give the picture back.

"Isn't he?" Nikki says, taking it from me and looking at it with longing. "I can't wait to meet him."

While Nikki fixes dinner, Justin and I sit in the living room exchanging Internet lists of names. As I pore over them, the baby's face hovers in my mind. I'm looking at these names through the filter of his countenance now, looking for a match.

"What do you think of the name Jaden?" Justin asks.

"I just saw that here. I love it," I say with a warmth that surprises me. "And I've heard it somewhere else, and loved it then too. Where was that?" I remembered and recounted it to him. "At grandma's eightieth birthday party a couple of years ago, I met the two-year-old grandson of the hostess: Jaden. I loved the name from the moment I heard it, and kept repeating it to myself throughout the day, not wanting to forget it. But I never once thought of it for your baby."

"I like it," he said definitively.

"Do you think Nikki will?"

"She might. She seems less attached to Ryan lately."

The subject moved on and so did the evening. Soon I was ensconced on my futon, lying alone and full of joy in the dark. Without meaning to, I'd let the name merge with the face. They belonged to each other now. It was a compelling, if precarious place to be. After all, I have no real say in the decision. But for the moment, that doesn't matter. Whatever his name becomes in the morning or next week or next month, tonight, it is Jaden.

April 6

I hear Justin get up early this morning and tussle with the dogs, imploring them to be quiet, but fall back to sleep; and when I awake, the house is still again. I venture into the hall and head for the kitchen to make myself the cup of International coffee that has been my rise-if-not-exactly-shine drink for nearly twenty years. I had just settled on the couch when Nikki appeared, her pink flannel robe tied above her belly, rubbing her eyes and looking like a pregnant five-year-old.

"Hi, Mom," she says, as she sits on the couch and nestles close to me.

"Wow, you're up early, honey." Anyone who knows Nikki knows how much she loves her sleep—like a good steak, as Bill Cosby used to say.

"Yeah, once I wake up now, it's usually hard to get back to sleep."

She starts munching Barbara's oat squares with me and I volunteer to make real coffee.

"In a minute," she says. "I thought I heard you and Just talking about names last night. Did you come up with anything?"

"Oh. Well, I'd told him earlier that Ryan seemed too soft with Bowes. It needs something with a little more punch."

"You know, the strangest thing happened a few weeks ago. I was talking to my friend Jane, and she started to say something like, 'Someday when Ryan's teacher calls you from school ...' and I almost said, 'Who?' It just didn't sound right to me. I couldn't believe it! I've loved that name since high school and suddenly it just didn't sound right."

"Hmm. That is funny," I say.

"So what did you guys come up with?"

"Oh, uh …" (You'd think an intelligent person could come up with a better stall than two single syllables.) I'm thinking this should be Justin's opportunity, not mine, but Nikki will wheedle the name out of me inside five minutes so I plunge ahead. "Well, actually, Justin mentioned the name Jaden and I really like it."

"Jaden," she says in an exploratory tone. "Jaden. Hmm. How would we spell it?"

I take note that my heart is beating fast. I'm more invested than I want to be. "J-a-d-e-n is how it's spelled on the list."

"Jaden," she says again. "I'll have to think about that. Jaden Bowes. Justin, Nikki and Jaden Bowes." This was a well-practiced litmus test, I could tell.

After I make the coffee, our conversation is interrupted every few minutes. "Feel this, Mom!" she'd say, placing my hand on her belly. "Oh, check this out!" Feeling the watery kicks beneath her undulating skin flooded me with memory—body memory of a time when another human being wiggled and kicked, bunched and dived beneath my skin.

When Justin appears from the hallway, Nikki says by way of greeting, "So, Jaden, huh?"

He smiles shyly. "Mom told you."

"She asked," I assert quickly.

"So you like it, Just?"

"I do." She turns to me with an expression that is pure punctuation. For months when asked about various names, he'd reply, "It's a possibility," in the most noncommittal of tones. But this *I do* was reminiscent of an altar-side vow, unadorned and without reservation.

"How about you?" he asks, standing behind the breakfast bar now, one hand on a cereal box.

"I think I like it too," she says. "Have you looked up what it means?"

"I'll go see." And forsaking breakfast, he disappears down the hall.

My heart is beating fast again, but this time from excitement. The air is rustling with anticipation, of being present to a moment of portend and posterity. Justin starts reading even before he rounds the corner. "Ruling with strength," he says and the scripture with it is, "You have given me the shield of your salvation. Your gentleness has made me great."

"That's it!" she cries. "Jaden."

"And it goes with Quincy too," he adds in grinning benediction.

The Naming set the tone for the day—a jubilant, giddy kind of day. "Merry Christmas! Love, Justin, Nikki and Jaden," she wrote on the kitchen white board with great flourish. "Oh! I love it!" she would exclaim periodically. "I just love saying it!"

In less than twenty-four hours, I'd gotten my wish: a name that made all the other names on the list obsolete.

Nikki and I launch into our organizing project with high spirits. We decide to start with confined spaces that will yield clear results by the end of the day. She works on sorting through her bedroom closet while I tear apart the large linen closet in the hall—but only after assessing the functions of each space per Morgensternian guidelines. Fortunately, the hall closet and her bedroom closet are only paces apart, as we constantly need to consult one another.

"Still want these old blue towels?" I'd ask, holding one up for her to see their true condition.

"Oh those!" she'd say with disdain. "Put them in the garage for car washing."

"Mom, come here a minute." I'd come. "Is there enough room in here to put some of those wooden shoe racks?"

We'd both stand back and silently assess. "Let's measure," I'd say with an air of old school confidence.

In the afternoon, we hit Target with a list and a plan, and emerge triumphant two hours later. Not only did we find what we were looking for, but our limited perspective has been stretched by Target's bountiful stock. Nikki found a wooden cart with doors to replace the open cart at the end of their kitchen counter. "So Jaden can't pull things off the shelves," she tells me, obviously glad for a chance to say his name. "And for more storage," I add, thinking of more immediate blessings the cart might afford. Anything that comes unassembled in a large, heavy box needs in my mind to be closely attached to immediate gratification.

It is midnight before the linen closet door opens, not on chaos, but on a functional work of art. Out-of-season blankets and flannel sheets sit on the highest shelf. Towels are organized by color. Pillow cases are neatly tucked inside the sheets they match, and white wire boxes (the devil to assemble) give divine order to linens *au current*. Below, smart plastic containers hold first-aid items, extra toiletries, and cleaning supplies. And of course, there is the as-yet empty box for *Jaden's* things. Thanks to Julie, we are zoned—everything grouped according to category. We have our inspiration piece behind the linen closet door. We have a baby with a name. We are definitely *in* the zone.

Mother-Daughter Team Wins Peace Prize for Organizing Feat

April 9

We've made all kinds of heady, invigorating progress. After another trip to Target, Nikki's closet—minus a dozen pair of shoes and the clothes she doesn't want to reclaim after the pregnancy—is ordered and workable. The guest bath vanity no longer holds strange, undecipherable secrets, and there is a lovely lavender bin for guest toiletries. It currently houses mine. The front hall closet has lost a few coats and gained a previously unused end table, which now houses doggie gear, gloves and hats in attractive muslin-lined baskets. The table games sit on the shelf above, wooing you from white wooden ledges. Justin seems to be intrigued with our process, asking each day when he returns what we've done, and nodding in earnest appreciation at our efforts.

And I'm quite sure that they're soon to name an aisle after us at Target.

Nikki has long conversations with her Mom each day, describing the process in detail. Ginny will be here at the end of the week for the shower, but somehow sharing it as we go seems important. "No, it's zoned," I hear her say repeatedly and with great conviction, and realize that Ginny has her doubts about our organization staying organized. That is the bane of organizers everywhere, of course. But that's where guru Julie makes the difference. Things aren't organized just to look pretty or neat. No, they're organized to function—to make sense to the person using them. They're organized on what she calls the "kindergarten model," a model where everything is grouped and everything has a place.

Tonight as we sip coffee on the porch and review our accomplishments, I suddenly remember the spark for all this renovation. "Isn't it amazing?" I say to Nikki. "Jaden started all this."

"I know. I just couldn't bring a baby into the house without getting things in serious order."

"He's what … about eight inches long and weighs a couple of pounds? And he's already got us working for him," I say laughing.

"I'm so glad I took the time off, Mom. I didn't even think about it when I made the decision, but we never could have gotten this much done if I'd been at work."

"It's perfect, see? You knew what you were doing when you took time off."

"I just hope I can go back next week. I've got to." "You will," I say, taking her hand. "Just be here tonight."

April 10

Today we started the kitchen. What can I say? Too much stuff, not enough kitchen. It has its good points of course, but no one can convince me that a person who cooked meals on a regular basis had much say in designing it. Nikki and I discovered a method of working together this week and it passes the ultimate test today. My job is to create the basic order and then she *re*-orders to suit her needs. As long as I don't get attached to my ordering—that is to say, remember that this isn't my house—it works beautifully. To our mutual delight, she has a mini-pantry in the kitchen now. And thanks to the miracle of wire shelves and turntables, she can actually see what she's got in every cupboard. Tomorrow we face a big challenge: the two shelves beneath the main countertop. They are deep, low, and loaded. Whenever you need something you suspect is loitering on one of those shelves, you must first decide how critical said need really is. And if the answer demands it, you must get down on your knees and go digging. I honestly don't know what the solution is, but the whole kitchy situation is dependent on improving that area. Target, don't fail us now.

I am a little subdued tonight when I turn off the light. The project is going better than I had imagined it would—not just the exhilarating improvement, but the quality time with Nikki. I even got a chance to talk with her about the whole labor-inducing issue and she listened earnestly. The prospect of sudden, fierce pain has that effect on her. Later her neighbor, Jane, with two induced labors to her credit, verified my findings. However I'm still concerned that Nikki believes that under normal, *non-inducement* circumstances, drugs can be administered the moment pain arrives. As if a first dose might be included with the registration.

I tried to impress upon her that labor has to get to a certain stage before they can give you any real drugs. She listened, but I don't think she believed me. Why should she? She's married to a person I gave birth to thirty years ago, and he's only two-and-a-half years older than the very last person I gave birth to. I mean, really, what would *I* know by now? I emphasized that I read this somewhere *recently*, but got the feeling that she prefers her own theory and doesn't see the benefit of giving it up for mine. I do get uneasy when I hear her speak of drugs so avidly, so eagerly, but I've said my piece. There are birthing classes for these topics after all, taught by people armed with both credentials and hand-outs. I await their exoneration.

I think I'm subdued for another reason too. When I first saw Jaden's profile a few days ago, I felt something move inside me—something reminiscent of that first fluttering of babe in womb. It was the feeling I'd been waiting for, the feeling that had been eluding me. And when I was present for his naming the next day, I was stirred again—this time with invigorating joy. Suddenly, it was almost as if I knew him, as if we'd already met and there was about to be a reunion. I had wandered down sleep's blurry path that night assured I was becoming a grandma at last—not just outwardly, but inwardly. But once I tossed my hat into the organization ring, that sense of connection began to fade. I became a woman on a mission, and found that I had to *remember* the feeling, conjure it up, instead of having it wash over me unbidden. I make regular visitations to the visage on the refrigerator, and though it never fails to amaze and move me, I lose the feeling as one loses water from cupped hands.

I'm disturbed and exhausted. Sleep would be an excellent choice. Why does sleep play hard to get when you need it most?

April 11

I was really dragging this morning. As much emotionally as physically I think. Nikki and I treated ourselves to breakfast at John's, the local no- frills, great-food pancake house. As we finish the meal, I all but plead with her to go back home and work on the guest room instead of heading off to Target in search of kitchen solutions. Her counter was sympathetic and persuasive. "I know you're tired, Mom, but if we don't at least get the stuff for the kitchen today, it's not going to get done." She is right. Plus, in the middle of her counter-plea, I realize that I am being outmatched by a woman who is six-and-a-half months pregnant. Which wouldn't be so bad, except that I regularly lift weights and power walk. I pulled myself together.

"Okay, but I'll need some serious caffeine. No wimpy decaf latte today."

Earlier in the week, en route to one of our many Target runs, we'd spotted a huge organization store. We'd bypassed it thinking it would be too expensive, but today, Nikki's curiosity grabs the steering wheel and thrusts us into the parking lot of *Storables*. Adrenalin outdoes caffeine any day, and this place is an organizer's rush. Nikki and I wander the aisles like two pilgrims who'd reached the Promised Land, pointing out one item after another, touching, admiring, and selecting. She finds a great make-up organizer for the still-untouched master bath. We welcome into our cart wire racks that would hold her bake ware upright instead of having to nest it. (That took care of one shelf issue.) And then—and you'd think we'd discovered a small country by our response—we find the answer to our biggest dilemma: that squatty bottom shelf, the one virtually good for nothing that you need to use (or remember you have) on a regular basis. Our answer is large, heavy-duty plastic tubs that come complete with tracks. *Easy to install! Takes only minutes!* For a total of twenty bucks and some muscle, two bins will gladly roll all that hard-to-reach stuff right to Nikki's fingertips.

Tonight, sleep will find me easily. The kitchen is done and I have an inordinate, but nonetheless, soothing sense of mastery. I was the official bin-installer since it required lying flat on the floor—an activity both forbidden to and unpopular with pregnant women nearing a third trimester. I was even undaunted by the fact that we placed Bin #1 too far back on the first try, allowing disappointing access to its contents. My muscles had a chance to strut their stuff after months of resistance training (and there's a *reason* they call it that)—making me feel not only competent, but pleasantly virile. "I couldn't have done that a year ago," I told Nikki, and though she patted me on the literal back in congratulation, it will be years before she understands what it means to say that at mid-fifty and steadily counting.

Jaden seems a little closer tonight for some reason. In the midst of everything else whirling madly around us—finishing the house, relatives arriving, the shower—I must find a moment to copy that picture. It is the true link to my elusive grandma self.

April 12

The house is done. My mother has arrived and Nikki is on her way to the airport to collect her Mom and sister. The forecast for tomorrow is Shower! I take this opportunity to wrap the gifts, showing each one to Justin and my mother first. On the top of the stack of packages, which alternates denim paper with a blue-and-white stripe, I place a framed picture of Justin at six-weeks old. He is on his tummy, head up, with that catch-it-while-you-can baby grin on his face. With my presents ready to present, the house ordered and zoned around me, and my son and mother softly talking behind me, I feel this incredible sense of wellbeing. Underneath, I know that my body is weary, but fortunately, it hasn't started listing its complaints just yet.

Family gatherings, as I've stated, are challenging for me. And that's when it's just my own family. Cross-family gatherings are a different kind of challenge. I turn a whiter shade of pale at these events—as in, I feel like I half-disappear. For one thing, the dynamics change between Nikki and me. I'm always conscious of stepping back when her family is present. It's as if she's been on loan to me, but now must be returned. She and I are close, but she and her family are close in a whole different way, a way that wordlessly takes precedence. It always feels like she's more distant too, but if I'm stepping back, how would I know for sure? But right now, it feels like time to relax into a new bio-sphere. Our families are soon to see themselves manifest in one little body—a co-mingling of genes never to be replicated. New common ground is rising up beneath our feet, and it is my resolve is to stand upon it with Nikki's family. (At least until Christmas.)

We're all meeting at a restaurant for tonight's dinner. Justin, my mother, and I get there before the others. The affable atmosphere of the Yamhill Grill seems like the perfect place to relax into my new, singular resolve. I may not feel like the insider here, but I've decided I don't have to play the outsider either. I've also decided that a glass of Cabernet Sauvignon will be my ally in this. When the three of them arrive, we greet with a round of hugs, and are seated at a large round table. Rounds are good. I think of Gavin's oft-used phrase, "Calling the circle." This circle has been called in support of Justin and Nikki, in celebration of their unborn child, in honor of family. The need for resolve melts away, and when my son offers a simple, heartfelt prayer over the food, I lean over and kiss his cheek, adding my "Amen" to his.

Our conversation is pleasant and light, centering of course on our shared, favorite topic: da baby. I'm not sure what Nikki's mother and sister think of the newly-declared name, but after starting out with Sarah, Jaden would definitely take some acclimation. The thing about names is this: once the person arrives, the name takes on a life of its own. You inevitably begin to associate that little being you love with that name, which given half a chance, transmutes the name itself. And lacking that, there's always nicknames. I suppose it would have been the same with Ryan. He would have become his own dear version of it.

When the bill comes, Ginny insists on treating all of us. Such a nice gesture. How is it that generosity so adds to the spirit of festivity—or is it the other way around? I've never treated a whole table full of people to dinner. I'm sure Ginny long ago lost count, and probably would never think to count. It's not that I'm miserly. It's just that such a gesture has never been within the borders of my reality. But borders are stretching it seems—if Nikki's profile and my upcoming change of status are any indication. So I decide I'm going to try it sometime. A whole table full. On me.

A week of full-tilt organizing has made me very decisive.

Baby Shower Leads to Future as a Dog Sitter

April 13

I head down to Jane's house half-an-hour before the shower to lend a hand. Talk about being out of my element. There are small children, pregnancies in progress, and party favors all in the same room. I start to feel tense, as evidenced by my glued-on smile. This is my automatic reaction to tension in public: smile harder. I think it has its roots in having my piano-playing-choir-directing-pastor's-wife mother for a model. Her security was galvanized to her smile. It's a habit I've noticed in myself, but haven't seemed to shake. After all, if you start frowning in public, someone is bound to ask you what's wrong, and then you're either going to fib or say something unseemly, like "Baby showers make me tense." Either way, smiling seems preferable. So I begin to make myself at least minimally useful to these good-hearted women who are giving my daughter-in-love a shower.

Despite my efforts, the tension remains throughout the afternoon, heightened by party games and lessened by watching Nikki open her presents. The tension peaks again, however, when my stack of gifts is chosen for unveiling. My heart even starts to beat faster. I don't know why this should be, but it's been true all my life. I even feel foolish trying to figure it out. It's one of those anomalies that hangs suspended in my psyche, resisting analysis. My only comfort is that the number of showers and birthday parties I'm likely to attend in my lifetime is diminishing with great rapidity.

My gifts are ribboned together in chronological order, which scares me a little, but is nonetheless an important part of the presentation. Symbolism has inherent order, I tell myself. My heart ups its little St. Vita's dance which I try to ignore in favor of looking urbane and composed. I am from California after all.

The picture on the top creates a stir.

"Is that *Justin?*" Nikki asks. I was pretty sure she'd never seen this particular shot of her infant hubby.

"It is really?" queries a nearby guest. "I thought it was just the picture that came in the frame."

"Me too," someone else says.

The frame *is* darling—faux silver with a three dimensional bear and rabbit in opposite corners. But a fake picture? Please. Frames with fake pictures go *inside* wrapped boxes, in which case, the gift is the frame. Only real pictures can outwardly adorn. (I know that verges on anal, but it also makes good sense, doesn't it?)

Next comes the set of Winnie-the-Pooh books, obviously vintage. And these otherwise nice women think these are fake too—that is to say, that I'd picked them up in a second-hand store.

"Where did you find those?" the woman next to Nikki asks me.

"And in such good condition too," her friend chimes in.

"On my book shelf," I reply, hoping I don't sound too smug. They seem genuinely surprised. Okay, first of all, here are the unwritten book rules: if you're giving vintage to a child, they must in the handed-down category, otherwise you buy new. (Unless of course, there are autographs or some other extenuating literary circumstance.) And secondly, why is it so hard to believe I had saved my Winnies all these years? Who throws out hard-bound Winnies? Maybe I'm better grandma material than I thought. I'm cheered at my prospects.

Next Nikki opens the little yellow suit. This really confuses the guests. It looks new, but oddly unlike anything you'd find in any store this side of modern day reality. The plastic liner sewn into the short little pants was made obsolete years ago by Pampers and its competing derivatives. When Nikki reads the note on the card, and realizes this was Justin's suit, everyone seems a bit relieved.

"Oh, you'll have to get his picture in that!" someone says.

"Justin or the baby?" another person counters, and we all laugh. Three down—one to go.

The last gift is the boom box. There will be no questions of vintage or authenticity here. This gift is merely strange. Original, perhaps, but not what you'd call classic shower fare. To their credit, people seem to think a sound system in the nursery is a clever idea and admire the CD's as they're passed. Thankfully, no one makes a showeresque remark about starting baby early on rock and roll, and the party moves on.

Jeez! No wonder I get nervous when people open my gifts. They have to be explained! If I would just go to Macy's and be done with it, I could relax and quit smiling like a fiend. Somehow inspiration always gets the upper hand and I end up feeling like a songwriter on open mike night—debuting gifts instead of giving them. *You do this to yourself* I tell myself, as my heart, relieved of its compensatory duties, begins to approximate its preferred pace.

After the gifts are all open and before my son is summoned to haul them two doors down, there is the familiar post-shower lull. A few immediate goodbyes, a few revisits to the cake table, more goodbyes. Then a couple of family pictures are snapped with all of us lined up on the couch as if waiting for a bus instead of a baby. And finally just a handful of us, all family except for Jane, who looks to be family herself. She's lean-ing affectionately against Ginny, marveling aloud at her own unabashed enjoyment of being mothered. *"Look* at me!" she exclaims more than once in exalted surprise, but doesn't budge from Ginny's side. I know this isn't an uncommon scene for Ginny or her daughters. Many of their high school friends, I've been told, called her Mom. There's something about her—nothing singular, nothing simple—but something essentially and corporeally maternal. I could feel the old insecurity playing countermel-ody to Jane's lilting satisfaction. Ginny would be the epitome of a real grandma: the kind water-colored into story books, the kind children the world over want. But Jaden won't be left wanting. In Ginny, I tell myself, he'll have the ideal grandma, the kind that genuinely goes with the name. The kind you nuzzle against when you're three or thirty. I start to slide into that feeling from last December, of being the other grandma. And then I stop. *To know this child and have him know you,* I hear again. It was the phrase that had snatched me from the jaws of neuroticism then and can do so now. There is no ideal, really, I remind myself. No perfect anything. There's just knowing and being known. Just loving and being loved. Ginny and I will go about those things differently, and Cindy will have her own version of it too. Perhaps together we will comprise the maternal embodiment of all things Grand.

When Jane's husband arrives home with their three boys, we begin to pack up the boxes and bags of baby ware for the short journey to its right-ful home. Justin loads the bigger items into the car and the rest of us make a cheerful and jaunty procession down Logan Lane with the cake leading the way. We quickly reassemble ourselves into two vehicles and drive out to the neighboring town of McMinnville. Sometimes I enter McMinnville, Oregon mindlessly—as if it's any other town. But on an occasion like today, I'm mindful. I won my very first competitive speech trophy at McMinnville College well over thirty years ago. And now I'm back to buy my first grandson's rocking chair. Life just makes you giggle sometimes. Like making an out-of-the way place a site of such momentous firsts.

Nikki has friends who own The Furniture Outlet in McMinnville, and thus we sojourn there to choose the perfect rocker. I'm glad to hear that she's already narrowed the choices down, and that none of them involve the nostalgic, but mean-to-the-body traditional rocker complete with spindles against spine. Baby is comfy either way I realize, but let's face it, his comfort is not on our minds as we each, in turn, try out the chairs—putting our feet up on the rocking ottomans and comparing the depth of the plush. Consensus is reached by virtue of color and design: the variegated blue one with the high, curved back and wide arm rests, wins. We're all envisioning falling asleep in this thing, I can tell. Hopefully not before baby himself. As the chair is loaded into the truck, my Mom and I decide whose plastic we'll use to make this shared gift to our great and grand child. With our task accomplished, we all unite in our hunger and head to Ruby Tuesday's. We get one of those wonderful long booths, and settle in three to a side.

I might not have remembered this meal or its congenial, hodge-podge conversation save one subject: dogs. Nikki had won a trip for two to Hawaii, a reward for her high production with her company. When the date for the trip had been released, it was in question whether or not she would be fit for travel in early May—just over two months before her due date. And because the prize of luxury accommodations on the Kohala Coast involved a company-wide conference, the date couldn't be altered. The obstetrician's nurse had frowned and wagged her head at the prospect, saying she didn't think Doctor would approve it. Two weeks later, however, he declared Nikki safe to fly without hesitation. At the table now, with Hawaii in countdown mode, the subject of dog care arises. Ginny and Sam are the usual suspects, having made a habit of keeping the dogs when Nikki and Justin travel. But at the mention of it, Ginny audibly groans.

"I'll pay to have them boarded," she says instantly.

"Why?" Nikki asks.

"It's just too much with Dad and me being gone all day. Not to mention what it does to *our* dogs and cats."

Justin doesn't comment, but Nikki and I both know what he's thinking. He isn't going to board the dogs. Regardless of who pays the bill, he doesn't board his dogs. And sitters had proved to be an unsatisfactory solution to the dog-care dilemma in the past. I could see the alarm in Nikki's face, her pregnant-perfect dream of Hawaii with her husband sliding away from her. It was several hours before I recognized the perfect solution to the problem.

When Nikki takes her Mom and sister to the airport, I broach the subject with Justin. "I could come take care of the dogs, Just. They know me, and it would be another chance to see you guys before Jaden's born."

"That might just work. Thanks, Mom," he says.

And so I leave the fate of a pregnant woman's hard-earned dream in his hands.

Third Trimester

Desperate Woman Succumbs to Internet Prowess

April 15

It feels strange to be leaving Portland today. On this visit I've bonded not only to Jaden, but to his parents at a new level. I've even bonded with their house, and can now effortlessly recreate its drawers, shelves, and closets in my mind like someone planning a robbery. "Well, no worry," I tell myself, feeling weepy and exhausted as I make the trek down the familiar corridors of the airport, "you'll be back soon." Arrangements have been made for my speedy return. Sidney, Dakota, and I will shake it up in Dundee while Mommy and Daddy do Hawaii.

Despite a few tears trickling down my cheeks at take-off, I am happy to let my own life come slowly back into focus as Portland grows smaller and Sacramento opens up its arms. It's not that my own life is ever lost to me. It's just that I have a way of trading realities when I travel, plunging myself into the alternate universe of someone else's life—and then being so delighted, almost surprised, when my own is still there, humming along without me. So it's back to Sandi and cats and unopened mail. Back to the warm, bright colors of my own house, the comfort of my own bed. Back to the lists and the errands and the astrology readings. Back to a place that for the first few hours, looks utterly familiar and oddly foreign at the same time.

And I've also come back with an agenda. I need a name. My grandson is one up on me.

April 17

I've quizzed my friends and searched my soul, but no name has made its path to my door. So now is the time of last resorts: the Internet. I always feel like I'm cheating a little when I succumb to the Internet for inspiration. It's fine for facts and directions and weather—all those things you couldn't possibly know by yourself. But for matters of the heart, it feels like admitting creative bankruptcy. Still, the Net seemed to work perfectly for Jaden; it may just work for me. I put "Grandma names" into the Google search engine, and of course, attract an obscene number of responses—most of which are useless. (I retract that. I now have two really tempting grandma-generated shrimp recipes, and another for a one-hundred-dollar, prize–winning chocolate cake.) Still, useless as far as getting myself named. But here's the truly heartening thing about the Net: if you have the time and patience to slog through more than your share of uselessness, and if you can resist excessive side-tripping, (recipes et. al) you'll inevitably strike it rich. The first site that rewarded me for my patience was namenerds. com. It began with a list of the most common names, something I skipped right over in my commitment to bypass the usual. The names from other languages intrigued me, and I could feel myself wanting one of them to work. But alas, I couldn't find the inner Babushka (isn't that a head-scarf?), Oma, Tita, Tu Tu, or Bomma. Later on in my perusal, there was mention of the name Mardi, which was reportedly New Zealandese. It sounded like a name a child might fashion from the raw material of Maridel, and thus it gave me pause. But not for long.

In another category, the site listed names that had sprung spontaneously from the lips of the young—either some version of "grandma," or some inexplicable concoction that no one, including the child, could ever ratify. In this category, I was relieved not to find anything that appealed to me and I'll tell you why. Talk about cheating! Take some child's innocent and endearing name for a beloved grandma and appropriate it for myself? Could I *live* with that? This particular category also reminded me of what Lauren had pointed out several months ago. So often, grandparents don't end up naming themselves. Unless, of course, they're willing to insist upon their *own* choice over the fetching originality of their grandchild. But after studying this category, I realized there's a darker side to this matter of letting the child choose. Let me bless you with a list of names that grandmothers are reportedly *thrilled* with because they were bequeathed by a babe they loved: Bop Bee, Gummy, Goggie, Dodo, Gom, Muffer, Ninni, Papoon and Pitty-Pat. In addition to such unsettling nicknames, I learned that grandchildren sometimes name their grandparents for obvious, but surprising reasons: the color of their houses or their hair, the names of their pets, the places they live—even the things the grandparents call them! Thus, there are in this world functioning and learned people known as Red-hair grandma, Blue-house grandma, Grandma Patches (the dog), Grandma Puddle (the pond), and Grandma Honeybunch (what Grandma called the baby). I have to tell you that the thought of being named after my cat or my hair is unsettling.

Then of course, I inevitably came across all the *au currant* grandma names: Nana, Nonnie and Nuni; Mamaw, MeeMaw and Mimi. They beat Goggie or Muffer, but not by far enough to adopt. Besides, trendy is not my true agenda.

Finally, I came to the category with which I felt a kinship: a group of self-named grandmothers. Women of great foresight! Women of obvious self-awareness! Women who *knew* what they wanted to be called! And here they are now: Honey, Marmie, Moogie, Peaches and Shi-Shi. This is the best of what conscious, creative choice has to offer? Ah, well, at least there is a Trekki fan and a woman of great literature among them. I'm sure Louisa May Alcott would be pleased to see that Marmie made herself comfortable in the 21st century. There actually was one other self-appointed name that I rather liked—not just in sound, but because it had personal connotation: Momalee. The woman who chose it, chose it for the same reason I would: her middle name was Lee. But alas, there is no use petitioning Nikki with this one. It has the same essential flaw as Mommadel, and I don't even like it as well.

Other sites and insights will have to wait. I've got that fuzzy-buzzy Internet overload thing.

April 19

I put the copy of Jaden's profile on the front of the fridge today, alongside the image of him in his cocooning days. What phenomenal progress he's made! The once-bursting chrysalis, barely recognizable as human, has opened into a visage that draws my eye almost every time I pass. It's not just that he's abstractly recognizable now—eye, jaw, chin. It's that he's recognizable as *someone.*

My own progress is not nearly as spectacular. I've done some budding and bursting of my own, yet even now I feel more awed observer than expectant grandmother. But there is still time. And under Jaden's watchful eye, perhaps I'll progress more quickly.

April 23

Back on the Internet today. I don't find a name, although I do find a naming tale that delights me. It seems there were two grandparents, who for reasons that weren't disclosed and I can't fathom, wanted to be called "grandmother" and "grandfather." Puts me in mind of Heidi, but okay. One of their caring (and no doubt secretly horrified) friends suggested that those were awfully big words for a small child to say. Why didn't they shorten them to "GM" and "GF"? As the story goes, they agreed, which is pretty astounding for two people who started out committed to old world formality and ended up with the initials for General Motors and General Foods. But again, okay. Now here's the really great part—which means, of course, that the child itself got involved. For all the effort that went into choosing those names, what came out of the mouth o'babe was not GM, but "Jim" and not GF, but "Jeff"! Don't you love it? And if you do, you'll love this even more: those names eventually morphed into "Jimmy" and "Jeffey." Perfection, isn't it? And these grandparents, who started out with such proper intent, reportedly love their given names. Which tells me that they were never really "grandmother" and "grandfather" at heart. They were Jimmy and Jeffey waiting to be outed.

Besides giving me a giggle and a cute story to tell my friends, who love it when I talk grandma, it gave me something else. Freedom from the search: the Internet, the brain-storming, my own inner list. I close the computer and walk out to the kitchen, placing myself in front of my grandson's intent gaze. "Hey, Jaden. I realize this name business is ultimately up to you, so just grant me one request: please don't call me grandma." I touch my finger to his nose and break into a grin. I think we have a deal.

April 26

Nikki's back to work and managing okay, but still longs to be at home. The trip to Hawaii and the beginning of her maternity leave are keeping her going, like two, great dangled carrots—or in Nikki's language, carats. She sighs frequently when she talks business, the way my mother did when she carried the burden of church work on her back like a Sherpa, a servant of others' dreams. As a child I used to ask my mother why she sighed. She didn't know. She didn't even realize she was. I don't bother to ask Nikki; we both know why. Increasingly, however, the professional side of her life is disposed of quickly when we talk. And then the sighing disappears. She grows light and animated as she talks about nursery furniture, talking-baby dreams, and Jaden's belly dancing.

I love the way the English use the pronoun "our" when referring to family members. It connotes such belonging, and seems to be used whether the behavior is deplorable or beloved. "Our Rose," BBC character, Daisy, will say about her flirting, man-chasing sister. "Our Hyacinth," she'll call her social-climbing, obtuse sibling. I never use the reference aloud, but sometimes, privately, I do. "Our Nikki, she's got it bad, wouldn't ya say, mate?"

Nursery Crisis Resurrects Inner Self Long Assumed Dead

May 2

Nikki calls today flustered and upset because the nursery furniture they ordered months ago is back-ordered and due to arrive (though not promised) shortly *after* Jaden. *No good.* Now she and Justin will have to put their compromising skills to another test: choosing baby furniture from what's in stock at Babys R Us. And since their preferences often run perpendicular to each other, fewer options do not help their cause. Fortunately, Brad and Cindy are en route to Portland for a weekend visit. So at least the frustrated pair will have interested and sympathetic parties to help them sort things out.

My first response, of course, was sympathy too. To have made an important choice and be expecting the results of it any day, only to have disappointment delivered to you instead, is upsetting. But after I hang up, I hear something else. I didn't know I felt anything but empathy until this disgruntled little voice inside me started muttering about "real problems" and "people with no cribs or without a house to put the crib *in*—or no baby at all." It's what astrologer Steven Forrest calls "the Old Fart voice": the one that invariably begins with the inflection, if not the actual words, "when I was your age." I grouse back at this gnarly little self.

"Okay, okay, so when *you* were their age you were mighty glad to get a second hand crib, is that right?"

"That I painted myself!" the voice adds.

"I know, I know. And matched it to your old blue dresser which took three coats of paint."

"That's right, and it was lovely. Plenty good enough. Kids these days …"

"Kids these days have choices and money," I say to this residual of the past, long-believed among the dearly departed. "And neither's a crime nor a lack a of character. So get off it. Admit it: you'd have liked nothing better than to go into a store and buy that baby a brand new crib with a dresser to match."

I'm heating up, ready to defend my young, but Ms. Voice is already gone. I lost her as soon as I cut off her rant.

I sink into my couch, pull up my knees and look for that *other* voice. The one I know is there underneath the genuine sympathy and beyond the comprehension of the annoying old lady. It's my truest voice on all occasions, but not always the one that rises first. It's this voice: *see what unfolds.* In its Pollyanna form it's a glib *oh, it'll all work out,* said with wave of hand and not much heart—a substitute for empathy. But in its deeper form, it's this battered and blown, yet still-breathing trust in the Process. *See what unfolds.*

I unfold myself from the couch, breathing deeply as I stretch. Applying this life-maxim to others is easy. Its self-application that takes pluck of spirit. Whether it's your first crib or your first grandchild.

May 5

What a way to spend a spring Sunday: brunch and theatre with friends! We gather at Cheryl's house for a feast of quiche, strawberries and champagne. We're rushed getting out of there, the way women are when torn between each other and matinee tickets. As we gather purses and platters, Cheryl hands me a bag. "For Mother's Day," she says with smiling eyes. I pull out the tissued bulge to find a small pillow the colors of my bedroom.

It's inscription reads, "A Grandmother listens with her mind, but understands from her heart." I'm surprised at my response. I'm not a person whose decorating persuasions have ever intersected with the world of sentimental pillows. Neither is Cheryl for that matter.

"I love it!" I say with genuine pleasure. "I love what it says; it's not that syrupy, sentimental stuff."

"Would I have bought it for you if it *were?*" she asks.

"And it's the colors of my bedroom, too!"

"Would I have bought it for you if it *weren't?*" she asks.

"No, of course not," I say, laughing as we hug. Cheryl and I have helped decorate each others' homes and watched enough HGTV Design Time Saturday Night together to finish each other's decorative sentences.

"Wasn't that sweet of her?" I say to Sandi in the car. "My very first Mother's Day grandma gift."

"And I have to say, you're taking it quite well."

May 7

I've never quite understood the saying, "Life imitates art," though I probably shouldn't be admitting that in print. And for the record, I have tried. Here's my motto: "Life imitates dreams"—and by dreams, I mean the kind you wake up with in the morning. A few years ago, I started noticing that I sometimes had real-life experiences that sounded more like breakfast table dream-sharing fare than something that would actually occur. Example: I am driving a narrow two-lane road on the coast with a fire engine bearing down on my fender, blasting its ear-shattering horn. I'm more than eager to cooperate, except that there is nowhere to go. One side is embankment, the other a drop of several feet. Dream or Reality? You Decide. (I nearly got hit by an oncoming car when I finally spotted and flew off onto a dirt drive on the opposite side of the road.)

Nothing quite that nerve-shattering happened at Nikki and Justin's over the weekend. But something dreamy did: there's a nursery now. Where just a few days ago there was nothing but stacks of shower gifts, a rocker, and a heap of frustration, there is now an assembled home for the newborn. The clothes, I'm told, are even folded neatly in the drawers. So the dream goes something like this: I dreamed that Nikki called, near tears, saying that the nursery furniture she and Justin had so painstakingly compromised on was on back order, and now they had to choose from whatever was available. The next thing I know, she's calling me and saying, "Guess what, Mom? The nursery is all done! We found the perfect set marked down at Babys R Us; someone had evidently ordered it and never picked it up. We both love it! The four of us had such a good time. Dad and Just put the crib together, and Cindy and I arranged the nursery and put all the clothes away. Isn't that great?"

The dreamiest part about this dream, the part that makes it float from unconsciousness to consciousness and back again is that it stars Brad and Cindy. Not the parents who live four hours away. Not the mother who flies in so frequently that she has enough free drink coupons to host an onboard cocktail party. No, it is the parents who because of work schedules and distance, aren't able to visit that often. It is Brad and Cindy, the least likely parents to help assemble the nursery, who became the perfect dream catchers.

See what unfolds.

Pressed-Board Sheep Test Edges of Decorator's Sanity

May 18

Off to Portland on my house-sitting mission, my last visit before the birth. I feel so heroic striding through the corridors of Portland International—so very *good parent* about it all. And at the same time, like a kid on Halloween, I'm counting my stash: no schedule, no appointments, little cooking, King's playoff games on wide screen TV, uninterrupted time to write, and unlimited *Trading Spaces* and HGTV. (P.S. Don't forget to feed the dogs.)

When we get to the house, Justin immediately escorts me to the back bedroom just as he did several months ago. No hint of the household dive remains. Instead a nursery of gleaming white crib, with matching changing table and dresser, anchor a room of blue and white checked gingham on bed and window. The blue velour rocker and crib hold bunnies and teddies who look pleased to have such plush digs. "It's beautiful, Just."

"It turned out nice. I thought the white might look too girly, but it's great with all the blue."

My eyes turn to the empty walls.

"We left those for you, Mom."

On cue, he opens the closet to reveal the shelves Nikki and I had admired at Target, along with the three sheep plaques and a cow-over-the-moon shelf she'd gotten at the shower.

"So I have a project while you're gone," I say, pleased to have my own contribution to make to the nursery—even if it will cut in on my commitment to leisure.

When Nikki comes home a few hours later, I get *her* tour of the room: the insides of the drawers, the hanging clothes by size, her ideas for the walls. Suddenly I have an inspiration. "Do you still have those extra squares from the wire boxes we used to organize the closet?" I ask. She nods and pulls them out of hiding. I stagger them across the floor as she watches in half-frowning puzzlement. "Fences for the sheep to jump over!" I say triumphantly as I lay the sheep on the squares. Her doubt turns to delight and she calls Justin to come look.

I will detest those three little white sheep and their little black noses in the days to come. And I will detest even more those white wire squares and my so-called inspiration. But for the moment, we're all beaming, nodding, and pleased as punch.

May 19

Justin wakes me at what is commonly known as an ungodly hour—which means it is still dark and evidently even the gods are "un," as in *un*available, *un*interested, and *un*der the covers. But I'm up like a shot. Though I'm not an early riser by preference or practice, there's always something exciting about big, early morning plans. And even though today's plan is mostly vicarious for me, I feel it in the air.

The drive to the airport is smooth and quiet across the dark, deserted Sunday morning freeways. Justin is pointing out landmarks, which I mentally add to the written directions he's already given me. Nikki intermittently remembers things I need to know: about plants and food, neighbors and mail. The night before I'd received Justin's tutoring on the dogs, the lawn watering, and the remote. (The first two were easy.) It's a pleasant, parting ritual: me as trusted servant, them as master homeowners. I enjoy the mundane lilt of it all, the conscious voicing of things they do day after day without much thought. But once I see the airport sign, my stomach starts to flutter. The goodbyes are looming in the pre-dawn light and it doesn't even matter that they are jubilant goodbyes, happy bon voyage goodbyes. There is something about letting go of children—however grown and capable and excited—that is still letting go of children. Never mind that I'm happy for them, grateful they can make the trip, and wishing them a glorious week. My stomach feels only the goodbye, and the ancient maternal fear of loss. We pull up beside the curb and roll from the car, Justin pulling out the cases as I hug Nikki, swallowing back the rise of tears. I hug Justin tightly too. "Have a great time!" I say as they walk away, rolling the suitcases behind them. They wave again and after they disappear inside, I hop in the car and cry. I miss my first turn and have to use my wits to find my way back, and by then I'm okay. It's not really that I'm worried about them or fear I'll lose them. It's just that goodbye. That eternally wrenching goodbye.

As I roll into Newberg, I notice that there's a crowd gathered in front of the new Safeway. "Grand-opening," the banner proclaims. People who've gone to the trouble to line up this early must know something I don't know, I decide. I pull in. I get in line and listen for the word on the pavement. I don't want to come right out and ask why we're all standing here at almost 6:00 o'clock in the morning. And when I do find out, I'm mightily let down. What we're waiting for is two tickets to a drawing and a free visor or coffee mug. I've been a city girl too long. I was hoping for pancakes. Or at least the coffee itself. Nonetheless, when the doors open, I stroll the shiny new aisles and enter Nikki and Justin in the drawing for a year's free groceries.

Back home—how quickly one takes ownership—I spring into action. I've brought my laptop with me, hoping to jump start the novel I've been working on for years and have been stalled on for months. To do so, I need a proper writing space. I clear the dining room table, remove one of its chairs, and roll the computer chair from the guest/computer room into its place. The chair is too rolly on the linoleum so I go in search of a proper mat. To my delight, there is a large rubber rug on the garage floor, with the name of Nikki's company engraved into it. Perfect! I sweep it and drag it inside, aware of how easy it is to appropriate the property of others in their absence. There's no "May I?" Or "Would it be okay?" Or "Do you think I could?" Surely it's a by-law of house-sitters everywhere that if you put it back like it was, it's permissible. Besides, my owners are en route to a luxurious resort in the Hawaiian isles. What do they care what I do with their rubber rug?

Sometimes the setting up is the best part for me. More invigorating than sitting down and making use of what my ingenuity has created. I step back and eye my new work space, and then notice that both the dogs are sitting at the sliding glass door eyeing it too. Hoping, perhaps, that the new configuration is on their behalf: a rearrangement involving expanded indoor privileges. Or maybe they're just curious as to what I'm doing with their property. More than likely, they're putting the new girl to the test. Seeing if their pair of cocked heads and earnest faces will induce me to let them in. I wave at them and sit at my new desk. The chair will have to be adjusted. I turn it over and spin it around for awhile before noticing that there is a little bar built in for raising and lowering purposes. I'm glad only the dogs are looking.

Once I'm properly adjusted, I turn on my laptop and bring up my estranged novel. This work has become a relationship gone bad for me—like an old love that you can still get misty about, but would walk a mile to avoid seeing again. I had thought spending a week with it in a new locale— the hope of every romantic—would stoke the fires of my once-burning desire. But as I electronically leaf through the pages, the only thing that happens is what's been happening for months: nothing. If this relationship isn't dead, it is most certainly in an impressive coma. And I get the distinct feeling that there will be no resurrection from either death or comatosity on this particular week.

I get up and pour myself another cup of coffee. Always a good ploy in the face of disheartening reality. Sitting on the couch, with my laptop blinking a few feet dead ahead, another light begins to blink. For the last few months, I've been thinking—casually, of course, just for fun, really— of writing a journal about the slow and circuitous path I'm taking to becoming a grandmother. There are others like me, aren't there? Women who forgot to pencil becoming a grandmother into their planners; who need at least two of the three trimesters to adapt; who may be slow out of the gate and need to know they'll catch up.

Without consulting my mind, my body starts to move toward the computer, triggering a string of sentences and a trumped up heartbeat. The dogs, who had lost interest once I started the coffee routine, are back. *What are you doing?* their frowning faces seem to ask. I wonder the same thing myself, but it feels too good to stop. I'm writing again.

May 20

I survey the nursery this morning. Here are the jobs I've been commissioned to do: 1)Attaching three sheep and their respective fences to the wall above the crib 2) Making an arrangement of shelves, pictures, and assorted toys on the opposite wall 3) Organizing the changing cart 4) General dresser-top, chest-top sprucing. I have a week, which seems like plenty of time, but I decide to start today. It may take longer than I think. After all, I'm writing a book on the side.

Step One: go to the local hardware store and do a little brain-picking. Hopefully some knowledgeable and patient hardware guy in this small town will take interest in my quaint little projects. Since the wire fences and the pressed-board sheep will be over the crib, I have to know they're going to stay on the wall unless the house itself falls down. My usual hammer-and-hope method won't work. As for the large shelf assigned to the other wall, it has two of those slots where the nails or screws involved must be exactly spaced and exactly level or what's screwed is you. This I have never successfully accomplished, but am sure it's just because I didn't avail myself of the utterly available: tips from the good old boys at the friendly, local hardware.

I dislike being out of my element. Often when I am, I experience what one of my former clients so aptly dubbed "getting the stupids," that is, unable to either communicate or comprehend in one's usual, intelligent fashion. In such a situation, therefore, I tend to rely heavily on earnest strings of "un-huhs." And so, en route to the hardware store, I mentally rehearse my request, being sure to underscore the part about the proximity of said wall to crib—and thus to the living occupant below.

Upon arrival, I look around for awhile, hoping some solution for sheep-upon-wire will magically reveal itself. When none of the standard hanging options apply, I solicit the help of an accommodating man about my age who looks perplexed as I describe wire squares and their relationship to

decorative sheep, but seems in the end to get my drift. In retrospect—
always with the retrospect—I would have been better served by bringing my
wire and wooden thingies with me, and perhaps making the crib scenario
a bit less graphic. He sells me wire u-shaped stakes or U-stakes, as they're
probably called in the business. They undoubtedly would have held the
wire grids to the wall along with a whole flock of pressed-board sheep for
generations to come if need be. Indeed, no harm would have come to the
child below—but oh, the poor wall! As I hammer the first one into the
unsuspecting plaster, which takes some serious pounding, a giant hole
grows to accommodate it. Only then do I vaguely remember the man
saying something about fence staples. I immediately dig it out with the
pliers and gasp. If I fill the wall full of these, I will have to mysteriously
disappear when it comes time to sell the house or redecorate the room.
Even with diligent patching, I fear that such a wall would be perma-
nently scarred. I'm not cheered. All I have to show for my first-day effort
is a hole that I must now coax some perky sheep into covering up with
its little pressed-board behind.

May 21

I'm not ready to face another hardware store today, so after writing for
a few hours, I decide to tackle the shelves. There are three. One of them
is a darling yellow and blue double-decker affair with jutting moon sides
and a jumping cow in the middle. The other two are small, scalloped-edge
shelves of soft yellow. The man at the hardware sold me a handful of little
plastic, crinkled things that look like play screws. I bet Playskool makes
something very much like them. These, he told me, can be put directly
into the dry wall where there is no stud and will hold a screw in their
centers. He's also the guy that sold me fence paraphernalia for a nursery, I
remind myself. These things don't appear to have any promising relationship to walls or holding things on walls. But I won't know until I try

The first step is to stud-search the wall. Only then will I know which kind of screws to use where. For this, I use the state-of-the-art stud finder that my son has left for me. It looks so much more capable than those little plastic things that could just as well tumble from a cereal box. This one beeps! It takes me awhile to get the hang of it, but eventually the studs are marked across the wall: exactly where they start and where they end *exactly.*

The next step is to transplant the arrangement from the floor to the wall. I'm armed with pencil, tape measure, a level, dry wall screws and their metal counterparts; and of course, a screwdriver. Mounting the household step stool, I hold the focal-point shelf—the bovine, lunar one—in its designated place with the level perched on its upper deck. I make light pencil markings on the wall: each of the four corners and across the top. Then I measure the two crude slots that are cut into the wood: down, between and to the edge. These measurements, with their maddening eighths and sixteenths, are transferred to the wall. Measuring shelf and wall again, I see there is a disturbingly small amount of room for error to hit the unforgiving slots. Disturbing because if I fail, I will need to find a way to improve on what are already my very best efforts.

My body tense, I step up again and begin to grind the first plastic tube into the wall, working hard to hold it straight, and watching it's bulky spiral eat away my precise marking and with it, my precious room for error. I then re-measure, making adjustments for the dry wall stud, and put the other screw in place. Lifting the shelf up with a hasty prayer, I start the awkward process of blindly trying to get the first screw into the slot. It drops in and I hold my breath, bringing the other end down onto the opposite screw. I hear a demoralizing thud as screw hits solid surface instead of targeted slot. Again, I use my fingers to feel behind the shelf as best I can. I'm off by the merest bit. "Noooo!" I cry aloud, followed by a bit of indiscriminate muttering. But I'm not about to abdicate. I jostle the first side, angling for any available space, tapping the second screw over just a bit to give it the right idea. And when I try again, the shelf slips into place. I stand back and survey my work. It's actually level. I'm exultant! I'm exhausted. After two days, one shelf is on the wall.

Thank God for NBA play offs. Thank God for children who have cable. Thank God the Kings are playing tonight. My shoulders are still aching from an afternoon of lifting, holding, screwing and pounding. I can use a legitimate reason to hoop and holler. Basketball isn't exactly relaxing, but it is nothing if not releasing. I take my after-dinner wine to the living room and let in the dogs. Might as well make it a party. It takes them several minutes to finish their licking, wiggling gratitude and settle down—one at my feet and the other in the bean bag. They look up dolefully when I clap and cheer, but they don't bother to bark in response. They've heard it all before and more. My son is a raucous fan.

At half-time I make coffee and poke around the kitchen for a cookie. I feed the dogs and let them out, then settle in for another round of the one sport that has managed to stay in my Hoosier cells. I grew up with high-school basketball mania. In my hometown of Muncie, Indiana, it was the stuff that headlines was made of. And even in the parsonage where I grew up, during the fevered pitch of play-offs, it was second only to church—at least in theory. In the vestibule before and after service, there was more basketball than God on most lips, but no way to tell which religion prevailed inside the sanctuary. I've laid aside so much of my Midwestern upbringing, but basketball, of all things, maintains a hold on me at play off time. It's a moment of arrested development, actually, a full-throttle regression into my past. The girl in her purple and white cheer block garb and the woman in chinos and a tank top don't look the same but underneath, the pulse rate, the elation, and heartbreak are indistinguishable. I couldn't possibly bear a whole season of this person, which is why she's limited to the play offs. Once in awhile, I can use a game like tonight, where the hometown boys prevail and leave me feeling that I, too, can beat the odds and emerge the victor. The Kings have given me courage to face the sheep again.

May 22

I didn't write this morning. With the nursery project so far behind, I decide to take the day to catch up. Instead of going back into Newberg, I head for McMinnville. I have a history of success there, after all. In this much larger hardware, I look first for smaller u-staples. The concept itself was good, just not the girth. No dice. It takes me several minutes to corral a clerk, who listens patiently to my dilemma, and turns the wire square over in his hands before handing it back and scratching his head. "Hmmm," he murmurs thoughtfully, making it clear that placing metal squares made for storage cubes on walls isn't something he's come across in the years of his expertise. "I have an idea," he says after a moment and I follow, hoping that fencing staples aren't the designated destination. They aren't. Instead, he hands me a package of little plastic loops that close with screws. "I think these might work," he offers. "Just wrap the loop around the wire and then screw it to the wall." *Easy for you to say,* I think to myself, but instead ask him to demonstrate. To my surprise, I think it will work too. In the check-out line, I imagine Justin and Nikki coming across the remains of these things someday. "Where did these come from?" one of them will ask. "What in the heck are they for?" the other will counter. It occurs to me that if my own life depended on it, I couldn't say what their true and intended purpose is either.

Back at the sheep ranch, I tackle the marred wall with renewed hope. The loops will be fairly easy to use, I discover, but not so easy to hide. What the sheep can't conceal will have to be ignored. Oh well. The wire fences go up on the wall slowly as I learn to place the loops in the just the right spots to avoid creating a sagging fence line. Once up, they meet with mixed reviews. Even with all my estimating and measuring, I have gotten them too far to the left, which means repositioning the sheep, which means they won't be where I'd told Nikki she'd find them. Oh well. Also, the white-on-white looks blah, with the wire making the wall look gray. Sheep to the rescue again. These little buggers are going to be compensating for a multitude of sins. Still, I'm pleased enough to call it a day, rewarding myself with a long walk and a nap before dinner, after which I settle into an evening of HGTV. A lot of reward for such slow progress. I'm living large.

May 23

Back to the book this morning. It isn't lost on me: this synchronicity of starting a journal about my grandpregnancy while alone in Jaden's birth home and spending inordinate amounts of time in his room. It does seem like the perfect launching pad for the writing—this odd, dreamlike mingle of caring for the dogs he will come to love, testing my wits and my patience on his first views from the crib, and cheering on the team that his daddy has rooted for since he was a kid. Somehow, I can be with the whole transition differently here: my changing role, my changing name, my changing identity. This process is more like the real change-of-life for me. Menopause, another thing the Boomers have brought out of the closet and changed attitudes toward considerably, was almost a non-passage for me. I read, I made choices, I was relieved of reproductive obligations. But this is the real crossroads into that other land: the territory of the elder, the world of generational shift, the tour de force of lineage. Now that I'm alone in Justin's house, Nikki's house, Jaden's house, the whole passage is beginning to feel like mine.

And so I write, partly because it is the thing this week was meant for, probably above all else. But mostly because I'm avoiding the wooly flock.

After a lunch of leftover grilled veggie sandwich, scored in McMinnville yesterday, I procrastinate by getting the mail, trying to hold a conversation with Jane (whose three children make it an entertaining, but unrewarding enterprise), and by watering the flower boxes on the porch. A nap is tempting, but could I really sleep with those three cutout critters lying in wait in the next room? Probably not. I march into the nursery, take a moment to admire the straightness of yesterday's shelf, and then face my charges. In my mind, sheep #1 will be angled upward, ready to leap. Sheep #2 will be actually leaping, and at the pinnacle of the arrangement. Sheep #3 will be coming back down to earth, looking as if he is about to land on the dresser. Sheep are followers, right? They will do as I command.

Here I elect to spare the reader the whole of the tedious and exasperating process that ensued. Suffice to say that the sheep had the same crude slots carved into their little backs as the shelf did. This meant the same torturous measuring and re-measuring from sheep top to slots, between slots and from end to end. And no, they were not uniform. Each sheep had its own personal versions of fourths, eighths, sixteenths and nubs of inches. Sometimes the wire got in the way of where the screw should go. The screws were barely long enough to go into the wall and still stick out far enough to go through the fake fence and into the backs of the sheep. And when with effort, I made it work, it didn't necessarily work because sometimes I was less than a nub off. Just enough to wound the sheep but miss the slot.

It puzzles me that I'm so determined. It's not my style to be so determined when I'm totally out of my element. Decorating is my element, a true love of mine. But the execution of it better be quick and/or simple or else I'm calling on the dexterous and handy. I did think at one point of asking Jane's affable husband to give me a hand. I did think more than once of waiting until Justin and Nikki got home. And it wasn't that I would have been embarrassed to do so because this project would be no piece of patty-cake for anyone. Even as I wrestled with the plaques—sometimes in tears, sometimes muttering sheepish slander—I knew that I was spending far too much time and energy for this to be simply about nursery walls.

When the three blue and white sheep are at long-last rising, leaping, and landing, looking as if they just jumped up there of their own accord, I smile, remembering an old phrase I'd heard as a college student: "Not triumphantly, but somehow."

And yet, in my own way, I do feel triumphant.

I sit in the rocking chair and stare out into the early evening sky. There is still work to do, but the hard part is over. And so it is with the process of becoming a grandmother, I realize. I can feel that I'm not finished yet, but I can also feel that I'm over some nameless hump. Within these four walls, and through my uncharacteristic determination to do something I don't do well, I have given this labor of love to my unborn grandbaby. I have given him a piece of myself.

May 24

Three more days until Justin and Nikki return. First order of business today: finish the arrangement I'd begun at the start of the week. I do so with high spirits, knowing it will be easy. The small shelves have forgiving brackets with lots of those little teeth, made for tiny bites of adjustment. They go up quickly. Next is an artful version of the Lord's prayer with pastel images in a blue frame. Then the original sonogram goes on the wall with the profile of Jaden's face on the shelf below, accompanied by small stuffed animals. My set of Winnie the Pooh finds a home on the top rung of the double shelf; on the one below, lotions and powders will sit within easy reach above the changing table. And lastly, the finishing touch: on the dowel underneath the shelf, I hang the little yellow suit.

This afternoon I spend on one of my favorite activities: prowling. I'm not an avid shopper except when I have a list and an agenda and then, I'm relentless. The primary thing I need today is containers to organize the shelves of the changing table as well as batches of small items that are currently running rampant in the dresser drawers: socks, booties, washcloths.

I find great containers at a variety store two towns away, along with powder and a few standard infant essentials: the obligatory plastic keys on a chain and a bumpy blue teething ring. For more serious acquisitions, I go to a large drug store and spend half-an-hour comparing the attributes of the various diaper creams and salves, selecting at last the one for sensitive skin. *As if some babies have it and some don't*, I muse on my way to the check-out line.

Tomorrow I'll be ready to finish my project and have a day to myself before the tanned, expectant parents swoop back in to reclaim their domain. Tonight the dogs come in again to join me for another King's game. This one proves to be utterly devastating, a loss that shouldn't have happened, yet somehow did. That's the glory and heartbreak of basketball for you. I return to Jaden's room, turn on the dresser lamp and soothe myself with prancing sheep, comforting gingham, and the tinkling of a musical teddy bear. A team of sweaty millionaires who came up a second late and a point short can't compete with this.

May 26

The homesteaders return late tonight and I'm ready. All the final touches have been put on the nursery, including a basket of stuffed animals and a soft stack of blankets on top of the cedar chest under the window. My home office away from home has been dismantled, with the dogs just as attentive to its demise as they were to its inception. The last two days have been relaxed: finishing the nursery, working a bit more on the journal, walking the lovely rural roads heavy with the scent and opulence of late spring, and getting my final doses of HGTV before I go home to my purposefully cable-deprived environment.

What started out as a favor to my children has become a greater favor to myself. I didn't know how much I needed to be here, to steep myself in this intensely pregnant environment. Even without Nikki's physical presence, my time here has been permeated with the unmistakable quality of expectancy: the room, the writing, myself. I cornered myself somehow in these last few days, cornered myself into finishing a frustrating project just because it was mine, and mine alone, to do. Cornered myself into making good on the idea of the last few months: to put this passage into words. And cornered myself—gently, almost imperceptibly—into the fact and the beauty of becoming a grandmother.

I'm thinking right now of a cartoon I saw when I was a young girl. A couple is on the way to the hospital for the birth of their first child. The mother-to-be is obviously and painfully in labor. "Honey," the cartoon husband asks, "are you sure you want to go through with this?" Like her, I'm too far along in my metaphorical process to turn back now. There is no going back, and after a week of doing little except immersing myself in the truth of the hour, I know I wouldn't want to.

I drive through the late Sunday night streets, en route to the airport. Unless it's obnoxious relatives who have foisted themselves upon you—or a distant spouse returning with even greater indifference—picking up is better than dropping off. I love picking up! When I descend the paved trail marked "Arrivals" and come around the curve, there they are, standing in the florescent glow of the airport night looking equal parts tired and happy. They've had a marvelous time I learn on the way home: pampered by Nikki's company, buoyed by their own adventures, full of exclamation and haphazard tales. "How was your time, Mom?" one of them asks as we near home.

"Great!" I say from the backseat.

"How did it go with the dogs?" Justin asks.

"Oh, we're pals. I let them in almost every evening."

"How's the nursery look?" inquires Nikki.

"Beautiful! I can't wait for you guys to see it."

"Did you watch a lot of *Trading Spaces?*" she queries.

"Some, along with HGTV—and of course the play off games."

"So you had a good time, Mom?" he asks.

"It was lovely," I say. "Just lovely."

And for the most part, it absolutely was.

May 28

As I walk the wide, elegant corridors of the Portland airport in pursuit of my ride home, I gaze toward the faces of the middle-aged women walking toward me. I wonder if any of them are arriving for the birth of a first grandchild. What would it look like, that walking arrival into a new stage of life? A wild and bodacious grin? Fierce concentration? Urgent striding? The polished sheen of joy? And more to the point, what will it look like on me, just six weeks from now? Next time I'm back in these corridors, walking the other way, it will be for Jaden's birth. I can't imagine how I'll look as I round the off-ramp corner and dive into the first restroom. Externally, all will be habit, cultivated over years of runs to Portland. Internally, nothing habitual. Nothing to go by. Nothing like anything else.

I hope to arrive a day or two before the birth. But of course all the strategy one can muster won't necessarily land you in prime time where the arrival of a first baby is concerned. It's ludicrous to plan at all, I suppose. What you're really doing is trying to do is match wits with a complex chemical process that no one even understands—medically or soulfully. To tell the truth, my only real hope of being there for the birth is Southwest's generous rescheduling policy. Without penalty, I can take more than one shot at it: scheduling, rescheduling, and rescheduling again if necessary. Of course, if the baby comes early, even Southwest won't be able to cheerfully help me.

When Justin was born, my husband, Brad, found himself in this exact dilemma. When he took a new job in Sacramento, I had elected to sit out the remainder of my seven-and-a-half month pregnancy in Seattle, unwilling to give up my base of familiarity, particularly my doctor. We sold our home and I stayed with a friend until my mother could join me. Then she and I moved into a furnished apartment for the last few weeks. Brad and I were on the phone every day, taking note of any change that might signal immanent birth. "First babies are notoriously late," almost everyone told us. "First babies take awhile to be born," others added to the chorus. But when an appointment with my doctor brought the news that the baby could be born any day—though his due date hadn't yet arrived—Brad hopped a plane to Seattle. He had just one week to be there, so this was a bold move on the part of our instincts. No doubt some of our advisors muttered to each other like oldsters do at the tracks, "Made the move too soon." But we were strangely confident.

Upon Brad's arrival, we went out for a romantic dinner in a French restaurant, and the next day to a doctor appointment followed by signing for the sale of our home. That night, right after Marcus Welby, M.D., as if continuing the story line, I went into labor. By dawn, we had our son. He was born quickly, the day before his due date, exonerating our gutsy call and giving us a week together as a family before Brad had to leave again.

I'm glad Justin himself doesn't have to gamble with being present at his firstborn's birth, but I'm hoping that some of the magic of his arrival will trickle down into my own story. In fact, when I think about being Grandma? there, it is Justin himself that comes to mind. I want to be there for Nikki, of course, but she has her own dear family. I want to be a witness to Jaden's first moments on earth because those will never come again for either of us. But it is for Justin most of all that I want to be there—whether it means exhausting my bank account, my body, or my last nerve.

I understand that some things just aren't meant to be. But I think it's okay to pray fervently and earnestly and frequently that this isn't one of them.

May 31

Nikki and Justin started birthing classes this week. Seems a little late, but then the shower seemed a little early. I guess it all balances out. I'm secretly hoping that the classes will broaden Nikki's perspective from her current focus of better-birthing-through-chemicals. Maybe even open her up to the possibility of breast feeding? Convince her of the folly of inducement? All of these hidden hopes, of course, right along-side my ever-diligent efforts to let go of control. I am making progress though, because while I still cling to certain wishes, they seem to be attached more like sticky notes and less like duct-taped directives.

Hearing Nikki's description of the class sounds so cozy: evenings where pregnant couples sit in a circle and learn the language and process of birth together, comparing notes over bad hospital coffee and stale cookies. And through it all, forming a temporary, but nonetheless, intimate club of the soon-to-be delivered. By contrast, I only have one memory of my birthing class, and it does seem to me that it was singular: *a* class. There were a handful of young, pregnant women and a presiding labor and delivery nurse. My only recollection is that she had us practice clenching our pelvic muscles for reasons that now escape me, and the story she gave us to make this exercise more what—realistic? entertaining? meaningful? was this: "Imagine that your husband is waiting for a very important call. He's asked you to be sure to answer all phone calls while he's at work. The phone rings while you are going to the bathroom, but you know you have to answer it, so you clench your pelvic muscles so as not to miss the call." By now phone machines have made this little scenario obsolete, but thank God, so has human progress. As long as you're going to be performing *urinus interuptus*, why not have it be for your own important phone call? There were no refreshments served either, by the way.

June 4

I've been waiting to see if the gentle, but palpable shift of my new identity as a grandma holds once I'm removed from Jaden's world-in-waiting and am plunged headlong into my own. It has, though not in a way I can describe from my head, not in a way language can access—but in that other way, the way of things shape-shifting inside you, softening their boundaries and yielding to new and tender forms. I'm still lacking the excitement I'm so convinced should be part of the deal, but here's how I know I'm gaining ground: when I enter that nursery now in my mind, he is there. Jaden. I can't see him exactly. Despite his now familiar profile, I can't imagine what he'll look like. But he is there. There's a little body in the bed, a presence in the room, the sound of breathing so sweet that it can almost stop your heart. He's becoming real to me. Could there be a better sign?

June 7

Nikki's been complaining of swelling the last few days. Not surprising given the equation: early summer + late pregnancy + stress on the job. But as it turns out, it is a condition that's more than the sum of its parts. This week's visit to the doctor temporarily terminated her professional life.

"Go back to the office only to get your things," her O.B. told her. "You're on bed rest." High blood pressure and borderline toxemia were the twin culprits. She called en route to the office to let me know what was transpiring.

"Do you want me to come?" I asked immediately.

"No, my mom's coming up early next week and Jane is two doors away. I'll be fine—it's not *complete* bed rest. In fact, if I can get the toxemia levels down, I'll be able to be up and around again."

"And work?" I ask.

"My maternity leave has unofficially begun," she announces with pleased authority.

I hang up and call Cheryl. It's been years since she's been a practicing nurse, but somehow she's managed to attain an impressive body of medical data and delivers it with unfailing comfort. "Nikki has borderline toxemia," I tell her. She takes the cue, launching into a simple and reassuring explanation of the condition, taking care to avoid the term "blood poisoning" that Sandi finds when she looks it up in the medical guide later. Of course, I'll also call my sister Linda tonight when she's home from her day at the hospital. She'll add another layer of insulation, protecting me from the hazards of my own ignorance and the worst-case obligations of the medical guide.

Then I picture our impatient, take-charge Nikki staked out in her bedroom for six weeks, and another fear arises: that old devil *inducement*! Once she's caught up on her daytime soaps, watched a few movies, and read a novel or two, she'll be chomping at the bed-rest bit. She wanted to be home, yes, but I'm pretty sure that included being outwardly and upwardly mobile, the continuing star of the Nikki Bowes show. This was not the stay-at-home scenario she'd imagined when coercing her pregnant self out of bed and into the early morning com-mute. Once that due date gets within arm's length, she'll be plotting the quickest route to drugs and deliverance.

Back to your mantra, I order myself. *Trust the Process. Trust the Process.* Then just for good measure, I pray that her borderline toxemia will never make it across the border.

CPR Teacher Doubles As Stand-up Comic

June 11

My CPR crash course is this weekend. I'm still having trouble imagining myself actually doing this. Maybe I just wanted to pretend I was the kind of person who would spend a Saturday at a Red Cross function as part of my grandparental duties. Maybe I was trying to impress my children. Or myself. Maybe I was afraid not to. My *raison d'etre* has grown as soft and fluffy as an unmanicured French poodle. Which is exactly why I made a commitment in the form of an online registration.

I haven't darkened the doors (something usually reserved for churches) of the Red Cross since I was a fourteen-year-old seeking to distinguish myself in the competitive world of babysitting by acquiring a bona fide babysitter's certificate. All I remember, and that vaguely, is a room full of other teenage girls and some faceless plastic dummies that didn't really want to be resuscitated.

I don't relish a reenactment. Yet I'm grateful that in a moment of sheer human lucidity, I signed on the undotted line. There are no refunds.

June 15

Nikki and I are spending lots of time on the phone. Chatting is one of her mainstays now, and I'm happy to oblige. Between her mothers, her sister, Jane, and some work calls, she seems to be managing her first week of confinement well. Next week her Mom will nurture and distract her, and perhaps on the next visit to her doctor, she'll be turned loose—at least into the neighborhood. The swelling already seems to be going down, she reports. "If this continues, I'm sure he'll let me drive a little bit; you know, at least up to The Coffee Shed for a decaf frappe." Even in confinement, a girl needs her ambitions.

June 22

I stop for coffee and a scone en route to the Red Cross facilities this morning. I've long practiced this habit of treating myself in the face of discomfort, uncertainty, or stress. Nothing terribly indulgent really, just a nice gesture of self-support. *Good for you,* the piping hot coffee is saying. *Atta girl* adds the scone. Of course if the stress is too great, I can't look a scone in its little raisin eyes without queasing. So I must be doing okay this morning.

Once there, I find the room and take a seat at one of the tables. Of all things, I've forgotten my water. I return to a wall of vending machines I spotted on the way in, but water is not among the selections. I have to settle for a lemon-lime soda. I haven't partaken of carbonated drinks for many years, but compared to thirst, I'm willing get reacquainted. When I return to the room, the teacher is there, running through the roster. She doesn't look like a Red Cross instructor, although if you had me at knife-point and my life was at stake, I would not be able to detail for you the appropriate look of a Red Cross instructor. Greta is her name, according to her nametag, and she is a pony-tailed woman of perhaps forty, with a strong upper body, a slight limp, and a German accent. If I'd known what a treat Miss Greta was going to be, I might have skipped the scone.

She starts by asking us to introduce ourselves and tell the group why we're taking the course. Almost everyone—or is it *actually* everyone—is younger than me. Parents, foster parents, day care workers, and people applying for adoption all give the obvious reasons for their presence. "I'm going to have my first grandchild next month," I say when my turn comes. No one intervenes with a look of astonishment or raised eyebrow of utter disbelief, so I plunge on. "I'm sure there will be times when I'm his sole caretaker, and should something happen …" Oh God, my voice is break-ing. *Why do they say breaking, as if you can go get it repaired somewhere?* I clear my throat and focus on finishing my statement. "… uh, well, I just don't want to be at the mercy of my ignorance should that be the case."

"Bravo," Gretta says and nods at the next person.

Should that be the case? I have a degree in English and I end up resorting to incomplete sentences and euphemisms like "should that be the case." What case? I didn't state a case. I feel half-formed tears at the ready and know that even if they don't fall, they will soon make my nose run. The next person is talking by now, but I don't hear her. I'm fantasizing about raising my hand and offering an explanation. *Wait! I hope you don't get the wrong impression of me. I'm not the sappy, teary type … really. As a matter of fact, I've had quite a bit of ambivalence about even becoming a grandmother. It's just that I want to do the right thing by my grandson should something …* All roads seem to lead back to this phrase, and my tears fatten, threatening to fall. I try to remember if I have a tissue in my purse. I try to focus on the fact that if the tears persist, they will all be wondering about a different *kind* of case. Everyone seems so collected to me, so calm—as if we've gathered here to learn origami. But I know that underneath, we're all struggling with a case of the *should-somethings*. Most of us are here of our own volition, wanting to be prepared for what we hope will never happen.

And Greta is about to rescue us all.

Perhaps you've been to Comedy Traffic School. But have you been to Stand-up CPR? Greta is seriously funny. She is funny without ever letting you think for a moment that she takes her subject lightly. She isn't poking fun at CPR, but she's keeping the morale up and the subject bearable with cracks about the inflatable dummies, the over-staged demo films and peoples' dire misconceptions of administering CPR. Her wisecracks artfully offset the stories of her own experiences on the front line, both successful and unsuccessful. "You think this is a crash course?" she says wryly when someone doubts they learn the techniques in a day. "Try learning it over the phone while the ambulances are on the way. At least this way you get a dress rehearsal." Greta is everything I'm not and I absolutely love her for it. She's direct, she's realistic, she's tough on details—and you're chuckling at every turn.

On the lunch break, I walk to the nearby La Boulangerie and muse over my sandwich about whether the Red Cross organization knows what a jewel they have in Greta the Ponytailed. I hope for a comment card at close of day to regale them with my comments. She would be one-in-a-million in the unlikely event of a million CPR instructors.

I order a post-sandwich latte and walk back to class, actually looking forward to the afternoon. Despite Greta's entertaining style and instructional savvy, I struggle with the next step: advanced dummy maneuvers. The dummies themselves are advanced too, by the way. They not only have faces and recognizable anatomy, but come in varying sizes that require varying procedures according to age and condition. And they even have the good sense to let you know when you've saved them! I have to admit that this is good teaching strategy. I also have to admit that it's not a life affirming experience when your dummy bites the dust. Greta intercedes of course, diluting the sting with an affectionate crack and adroit course correction, assisting me until my victim rewards me with proper inflation and glowing health.

By the time she passes out the exams at the end of the day, I'm still not sure I could do what's necessary in a crisis. However, I have my comforts: I pass the test, walk away with a plastic-coated, illustrated fold-out of procedures for every unwanted occasion, and should I end up on the phone while waiting for an ambulance, I won't be starting from scratch. I can also repeat the class, I remind myself—which I wouldn't mind a bit if Greta was in charge.

June 23

The plane to my mother's home in Boise got re-routed through Seattle today, where I spent a long sit-over—no laying is actually involved now, is it? It happens to be Father's Day and I'm unexpectedly hanging out in Justin's city of birth. I like the synchronicity of that, but like a lot less the fact that I'm making his first Father's Day call standing up at a phone booth in a noisy airport. In fact, right by a bank of windows with roaring planes in full view. There's something about raising your voice to express personal sentiments (with a finger in your other ear) that's hard to pull off effectively. "I *SAID*, 'I KNOW YOU'LL MAKE A WONDERFUL

FATHER.'" Good thing I sent a King's bib and a card.

Then Nikki comes on the line. "Mom, wait 'til you hear this dream," she says with a mix of wonder and alarm. "I dreamt that I was on a table in the delivery room, and all of a sudden the baby popped up out of my stomach!" I know the twin postscripts that will follow: P.S. "Isn't that weird?" and P.P.S. "What do you think?"

I don't want to say what I think. It's the thing anyone would think, isn't it? One word: *caesarean*. I stall, scanning for some other meaning the way my cell phone searches for service, its tiny magnifying glass roaming the lighted screen. But I don't pick up a signal, and have to say the word I don't even want to hear.

"I don't really want to say this, Nik, but it makes me think of a caesarean." Before I can foray into other less honest possibilities, she responds: "That's what I think too."

"Then again, you know dreams," I add quickly, "maybe it has to do with your *fears* of a caesarean. You think?" I can hear the plea in my voice, and though Nikki probably hears it too, she doesn't capitulate.

"No, it feels more like knowing something. The thought of a caesarean doesn't scare me."

The line is silent, in that way that only telephone lines can be. Like an empty parentheses that no one can fill.

"Well," I say, beginning to feel my body sway in the winds of unwelcome news, "we'll see, I guess, huh? I mean, I hope we're wrong, but ..."

"We probably aren't," she says finishing my unwanted thought. "In a way, I wouldn't really mind. No long labor with all that pain."

"But, honey, it's a harder recovery from a C-section and ..." I stop myself, realizing that this really isn't the time to list the disadvantages of what might be the inevitable.

"I just want Jaden, Mom," she says. "I don't really care how I get him."

After we hang up, I spin. Odd bits of information about the detriments

of a caesarean delivery pester me like whining mosquitoes in the night. I
keep waving my mental hand at them, swatting and covering my head, all
the time knowing that the only solution, whether in the physical or mental realm, is to turn on the light. I resist for the same reason I resist in the
night: I would have to fully wake up. Wake up to the fact that what I can't
swat away, ironically, is the feeling in my *gut*—the feeling that the dream
is prescient, just as her dream of having a boy was. Nonetheless, I take at-
tempted refuge in the familiar land of symbolism. Maybe the dream is just
about Nikki wanting to get the birth over with, or have an easy labor, or
avoid labor altogether. Maybe. Could be.

I'm beginning to think that it's easier to give birth *yourself* than to stand
on the sidelines of what appears to be "someone else's" destiny. When those
people are your children, that's an optical illusion of the first magnitude.

As I sit in the crowded airport, oblivious now to the noise and commo-
tion around me, I remember something I don't want to remember. Something I didn't take very seriously at the time. Something Nikki said to me
on the phone just last week.

"Mom, it feels like the baby's kicking in the wrong place for the last few
days. Like he's standing on my pelvic bone and doing a little dance."

June 25

I found the perfect frame for Jaden's profile in Boise today. It's white
wood with blue inscription. It simply says, "The first time ever I saw your
face …" More than just giving his wise visage a home, it will frame for me
that transforming moment between kitchen and dining room, between
heaven and earth. That moment when I leaned all the way into falling.

June 26

Call from Nikki today. An ultra-sound has revealed Jaden's true station
in life: upside down. Though I'm sure he's in a perfectly peachy spot ac-

cording to him, it's not one that's conducive to normal delivery. And at this point, there's precious little room for relocating in the hallowed and narrowed halls of Camp Mama. The doctor evidently felt obliged to offer the option of a painful, and by-the-way-not-terribly-successful, procedure of attempting to turn the baby. No takers there. And no wonder either.

The dream looms large.

Fetus Pulls Prank on Seasoned Doctor

June 27

"All this time I thought the baby's head was down—and it was really his rump!" This exclamation of the doctor, lost in the aftershock of yesterday's announcement, comes back to me this morning as I float on that ephemeral raft between sleeping and waking. This is an experienced doctor as I recall, a veteran moving toward obstetrical retirement, and Jaden put one over on him. I come awake smiling, oddly comforted at the thought of a prenatal prank.

June 29

Back home tonight, I take Jaden's profile from my dresser and put it on my bed stand. His will be the last face I see at night, the first I see in the morning. And in this simple ritual is my day-long, night-long prayer, my dedicated trust that Jaden and God know what they're doing.

July 1

Nikki reports today that she and Justin tried another method of turn-the-babe last night, one suggested by their birthing class teacher. Nikki really wasn't game, satisfied as she is with the portent of a C-section, but she accommodated Justin, who isn't ready to abandon the possibility of a natural birth just yet. It sounds like a much gentler version than

Western medicine's for-the-Amazonian-only method. The basic idea is this: drive the unruly fetus away from his current stronghold and entice him toward the desired spot. To this end, clapping and loud, discordant music is played at the upper end of the mother's body, accompanied by cold compresses on her upper abdomen. Message: the upper abdomen is an unfriendly, annoying place. You might want to visit, but you wouldn't want to get stuck there. But look! More pleasant experiences abound in the nether land. Soft, alluring music awaits. A loving voice calls your name. No cold vibes from nasty compresses. Message: you'll really like it down here. Come visit. Come check it out. Here, baby, here.

To be effective, they were told, this ritual would need to be performed consistently several times a day. Nikki, as it turns out, was only good for one experimental try. It seems that she didn't care for the jarring music, loud clapping, and cold compresses herself—and neither was she motivated to keep subjecting herself to them. So Mr. Jaden, who certainly wasn't going to fall for one introductory demo, is still happily ensconced in his rump-first position. That's his story and, as the saying goes, he's sticking to it. Perhaps literally.

July 5

Nikki called with the results of the second ultra-sound today. To "upside down" has been added the descriptor of "cross-ways." No wiggle room for a medical decision now either. Jaden will be born by cesarean.

So it seems that Dr. Duran isn't the only one on whom my grandson has pulled a prank. He's done a number on me as well. All these months I've been fretting about an induced birth that might heighten the chances of a caesarean, prompted by the impatience of the human hostess. Evidently I didn't need to be concerned about that. It seems that my grandson is in control. From his vantage point of upside down and cross-ways, with no room or inclination to reconsider his position, he is calling the shots. He has ruled out an inducement and is skipping straight to the Big C.

And this, I find, I can live with.

July 6

Jaden's birth is officially on the calendar: Monday, July 15. In planning the strategy for the occasion, our man of the womb has simplified everything. I confidently make my plane reservations today. I will, indeed, be present at his birth. I suppose there's always a chance that labor could begin early and suddenly set everything into fast forward, but somehow I don't think so. The guy seems happy exactly where he is.

July 9

In the past few days, I've said my last grandma-less goodbye to my friends Cheryl, Sherrie, and Lauren. Each were solicitous and warm, excited for me. "Call me," they all said, with that glow of impending good news. "I will," I responded, feeling the measure of love in each bond as they hugged me goodbye, sending me off to find my place in the land of Grand.

But when I am alone again, without the warmth of their excitement igniting mine, I notice that my own candle is burning low. This is more than a little confounding. After having turned my share of corners in the last almost-nine months, I expected to be feeling … feeling … *more* at this point. After all, I sent ambivalence packing some time ago, didn't I? Most of my fears have been packed away by now too, showing themselves for the useless, vacuous things they are. And that face—that face!—that sits by my bedside now, beckoning me to know him. Wouldn't life seem woefully incomplete without his newborn presence? Yet now that it's almost time to get *myself* packing, I'm missing the company of the companion I desire most: the shimmering goddess, Excitement. In what can safely be called the eleventh hour, she eludes me. And I don't know why.

Hospital Attempts to Edit Script of Birth Drama

July 1

Just minutes before students start arriving for my in-home astrology class tonight, Nikki calls. "Mom," she says, in that wrenching way that makes your heart pole-vault into your throat, "they've prolonged the birth two days. Wednesday instead of Monday!"

"Honey, *why?*" I ask, relieved that the news wasn't worse, but neverthe-less crestfallen for her reasons and for my own. "I don't know why. I just got a call from the hospital and they said it had been rescheduled. They didn't say why."

"Nik, call your doctor's office and find out what's going on. Maybe there's been a mix-up or something. Call the nurse there, okay?"

"I don't want to wait 'til Wednesday," she cries. "I've been counting the days!"

"I know, honey, I know. I've got to go, but promise me you'll call, okay?"

She promised, and I taught. It was one of those classes where the people in front of me, ensconced on my sectional in their long-ago declared plac-es, probably didn't get my very best. My mind kept straying intermittently from the agenda before us to my own reasons, astrological and otherwise, for wanting a Monday birth.

Plane rescheduling is the first, and least, of the issues. The second snag is a sentimental one. Monday is my elderly aunt's birthday, and she is excited about Jaden's birth coinciding with hers. But the biggest snag for me is lunar.

As an astrologer, I will tell you that all moons, which are symbolic of your needs and feelings, as well as your basis of security, are equally valu-able and honorable. And I will mean it from the bottom of my professional heart. But as a prospective grandmother, I have my druthers. Monday's moon is full of charm and relational savvy; not without its drawbacks, but easily lived. Wednesday's moon is stormy and complex; not without its considerable merits, but more demanding to all concerned. By the end of class, assisted by a dose of synchronicity, I'd come to terms. Geri, a student who possesses the same stormy moon in question, sat directly in front of me—a whole human being, not just a moon. A warm, insightful human being whose penetrating questions and considerable depth make her the person she is. Besides, isn't my pact with Jaden and God to trust what they are up to? Maybe a changing of lunar guard is part of the Plan.

As soon as the house is empty again, I call Nikki. The birth has been rearranged for Monday with as little ceremony and explanation as it had been unarranged. "I called the nurse, crying, and told her my family had all made arrangements to be here Monday, and how upset I was. She said she'd find out what was going on and call me. When she did, it was back on for Monday!"

I could see Jaden hanging out, using his mother's pubic bone for a rump rest, wondering what all the fuss was about.

Later that night

Standing in front of my closet, the open suitcase behind me, I contemplate what one wears to a birth. Perhaps I could have bought something for the occasion, but it's too late for that now. I pack one outfit, then reconsider, oust it from the suitcase, and choose another. This one is a long, soft yellow shirt over white knit pants and ribbed sleeveless top—what my friend Sharyn calls my "Hampton ensemble." It's comfortable and cool, the kind of classic look that won't reduce my grandson and me to tears of laughter when he's in his teens. The hair—now that's another issue. What's classic and chic in one decade is almost always a laughing matter in the next. My hair is on its own.

My suitcase is packed, awaiting only the addition of my cosmetic bag in the morning. I lie awake in the dark, thinking about all the runs I've made to Portland. Taking Justin to college. Helping him find an apartment as a senior. Transporting furniture to said apartment. Visiting Nikki and him at school when they were dating. Visiting them (and their dog Sid) after they'd gotten engaged. Staying with them as newly-weds—and watching Justin mow a lawn of his own volition for the first time. Trips for Thanksgivings and a Christmas, an occasional birthday, and sometimes just because it had been "too long."

But none of those trips, taken in various states of mind and heart across ten years, can compared to this one. They were about miles and milestones. This one is about creating generations, lineage, and history. This one is about gathering around the manger of a hospital cradle and being witness to the blessed and endless unfolding of genealogy. This one is about the never-look-back transformation from couple to family, from parents to grandparents, from here to eternity.

And it's also about the transformation of every part of me: the woman, the person, the mother, the friend, the astrologer, the soul. Changed forever whether excitement runs fast enough to catch up with me or not.

Bathroom Stalls Serve As Decompression Chambers

July 11

I'm up early this morning, doing all those last minute things that seem to multiply in the night. Sandi, whose work takes her out onto the highways and byways early every morning is there to say goodbye. I'm disappointed when she gives me her standard farewell of "Have a good trip!" I was expecting something more, but for the life of me, can't imagine what it would have been. "Have a good baby?" "Get excited!" *What?* She, who has been so characteristically patient through this whole thing, is probably relieved to have it culminate, and at 5:30 in the morning, is no doubt equally relieved that I appear to be siding with my saner self. Once in the shower, I realize that I was wanting her to compensate for my own lack of excitement, to do or say something that might shift me into joy, or at least a dose of giddiness. Not her style. And not her job, either.

I also notice my legs as I shave them in the steam. Veins of the pre-ver-icose variety have bloomed on them! When? Has it been that long since I shaved my legs? Or looked at them? I've got grandma legs! Does this come with the package, built into the process? *"What?"* I say aloud, touching them to make sure they're real. *"What?!"* And then, to my surprise, I dis-solve, not into tears, but laughter. Excitement has yet to possess my body, but grandma veins are Johnny-on-the-spot.

When Margaret knocks on the door, I'm ready, though just barely. "Are you feeling excited?" she asks, looking the picture of it herself. "

I don't know what I'm feeling, really."

"It's okay," she assures me. "You will."

En route to the airport, we chat about the pros and cons of caesareans (Margaret is a credit to Virgos everywhere with her storehouse of pertinent and surprising facts), about when I'll call her with the news, and when I'll be back. "You'll be in my prayers, all of you," she says as she hugs me at the curb. And then I'm off, shouldering my flight bag and towing my luggage behind me and my newly-sprouted veins—straightaway into the next world.

The plane ride is uneventful and dispassionate. I could be going to any old thing according to my emotional gauge. Maybe if I would have sat by some kind woman a little older than me, who happened to ask what was tak-ing me to Portland, I could have burst into smiling tears half-way through my answer. Instead, I stride off the plane as usual, head for the first restroom between me and my waiting baggage, sit on the porcelain furniture, and sob. It isn't a matter of *no* feelings, I quickly see, but a matter of *many* feelings kept at bay without even knowing there was a bay. I emerge with a lighter step, and to my delight, detect a flicker of excitement. I walk the corridors relieved. It isn't just my body arriving in Portland. I've come along with it.

Justin picks me up outside the terminal, and quickly tells me the plan. Nikki is home waiting to go to dinner, but this is his best chance to get a gift for her. He wants to give her an Italian charm bracelet as a commemoration of Jaden's birthday. We go to Lloyd Center and find the kiosk, choose a bracelet and three charms: blue baby footprints, a cross, and a dolphin, the latter in commemoration of her recent Hawaii-kissed swim with those magnificent creatures. My own necklace, recently-turned-anklet for Nikki, dangles in my mind—the gift his father gave me when Justin was born. Is this real? Is this how quickly it all goes? One minute you're the recipient of a lovely, sentimental gesture—and the next, you're browsing kiosk-ware with your thirty-year-old father-to-be?

It's not good to keep a hungry pregnant person waiting for her dinner, which is exactly what Nikki tells us when we call from the car. She'll meet us in town, she says, to speed things up. En route there, as Justin and I ride along, an utter contentment slides over me. We talk about the baby, the birth, the things he wants to get done, how long he's planning to be off work. And between each subject, in that pause, the contentment shuffles back again—never really gone, but still returning. It lasts through dinner, through the drive back to their house, and as I'm putting my things away. Then Nikki calls to me to come with her down to Jane's.

I don't remember ever seeing Jane that night, actually. What I remember is a friend of Jane's, encountered on the sidewalk in the process of our departure. When Nikki introduces me as Justin's Mom, the woman cocks her head and elevates her eyebrows.

"So the mother-in-law, huh? A little aloof … a little distant." Even said with a hint of humor, it was jolting. Still I managed to respond.

"Not really," I say. "We don't have the typical relationship at all." And then I waited for Nikki to back me up—to put her arm around me and speak her line in my script. "Mom and I are really close," she would say. "She's one of my best friends."

Had Nikki not heard? Why wasn't she responding, rushing in to back up my protestations? She said nothing and the conversation moved on, though of course it did so without me. I stood there feeling embarrassed, hurt, and ridiculously sensitive.

Nikki is days away from giving birth to her first child, I told myself in bed that night. For all you know, she didn't even catch what was said. She hasn't changed her mind—she loves you. And besides, you're not just a big girl, you're an old girl, and this is beneath you. Let it go. All true; but still, I cried into the futon that had by now become my comfortable and comforting pal.

July 12

I awake feeling renewed. Some contentment has leaked out, but can no doubt be replenished. The three of us drive to McMinnville for breakfast at a new café, the Wildwood. The menu features "Crunchy granola french toast" and "Savory breakfast potatoes." And the walls, covered with 50's memorabilia, entertain you while you wait. (Especially if you actually remember when all that stuff was in your life instead of on the wall.) With a start like this, the day clearly is in a mood to meander and we are willing to oblige. We watch episodes of *Trading Spaces* on TLC, go into town for mocha frappes, and sit outside together with Nikki soaking in her neighbor children's turtle pool and me beside her, reading.

Throughout the day, I snap pictures for a future project I'm hatching. Remembering how much children love to hear about when they were born, I hit on the idea of an illustrated version. So I'm taking photos in these days leading up to Jaden's birth, which I'll laminate and put on a large metal ring—thus supplying him with his own hands-on story of his arrival in the world. Mommy in the turtle pool is sure to make the cut. By late afternoon, I finally work up some ambition and whip up a batch of chicken enchiladas for dinner.

Nikki and I sit on the porch tonight and talk about possible names. This time I offer Mimi, not because I am smitten with it, but because it seems like a derivative of Maridel and easy for a small child to say. Nikki doesn't take to it, which gives me a good excuse to drop it as well.

"Maybe I'll just be Grandmadel," I say, speaking the name aloud that I've been pondering for awhile.

"Or maybe just Delly," she counters with a wink. "Hey Jaden, let's call her Delly," she says, dipping her head stomachward.

We laugh together in the summer night, and by the time we head inside, the contentment bag is overflowing.

July 13

The day after tomorrow. It was a phrase that, as a child, made waiting until Christmas or my birthday—or later, until a reunion with my boyfriend or my wedding day—bearable. If it was "two days away," it was too long, too agonizing. But if it was the day after tomorrow, it was close enough to touch. It was closer than you thought.

On *this* day after tomorrow, we head to John's for pancakes. Perfect day-after-tomorrow choice. John himself in the kitchen, turning out home-cooked food that creates standing-room-only by 9:00 AM on this, and every other weekend. The three of us score a booth after waiting only about ten minutes, and settle in, giddy with relief and bustling enzymes. With Jaden's birth in easy reach, we are becoming incapable of talking about anything else. This morning, we manage, as long as the menu is in front of us, to talk about breakfast fare, particularly the pros and cons of pancake vs. omelet (it's a home fries issue). But once the menus have been happily rendered useless, it's as if Jaden, sitting there with us (albeit incognito), has taken over our minds again. We're down to incidentals by now, of course. All the big ticket items have been taken care of. Now it's talk of that one last thing to shop for, the time of the blood test today, washing a few more undershirts and onesies. It doesn't have the air of discussing incidentals at all, though—none of the boredom of the usual details. There's a sheen to this conversation, and a sly grin that slithers from one face to another. This is the camaraderie of people in love with the unseen. Everyone else here is just having breakfast. We're putting finishing touches on destiny.

After breakfast we make a trail through the cluster of still-waiting patrons, their hungry faces eyeing our littered corner booth. Back home, with Nikki settled outside in the late morning sun, I start on the wash of things so small they evoke the memory of the tiny apartment-sized appliances in which Justin's first clothes were washed and dried. They were the perfect size for garments so small, almost like doll clothes in play appliances. In this washer, it would take a hundred of these bitty things to make a decent load. While they slosh away in their own soapy world, I unload the dishwasher. Justin is making a run to the dump, releasing all the things that lost their happy hiding places in the interest of clearing the decks to make more space. I'm alone in the house, pulling still-warm dishes from their slots, listening to the clothes moving through their cycle, but none of it is ordinary today. Everything I do, even lifting and placing dishes, seems to be preparation now, sweet and almost holy. Or is it this: that what is holy all the time—the sacredness of life and of the present—is utterly available now, undisguised and breathable? My eyes keep lifting to Nikki, to her napping, lovely form, quiet in the sun. Even without her in it, the whole house is pregnant.

In the afternoon Justin prepares without knowing it, for a long string of Christmas Eves to come. His assignment: turn the assorted bagged and jangling contents of a heavy carton into a fully functioning item. In this case, a stroller. Meanwhile, Nikki and I head out for the final errands—if getting blood drawn can be considered an errand. I suppose it qualifies as long as it's not my arm sporting a rubber tourniquet. Even this proves to be a bit festive though. The woman at the intake desk asks about the baby's name, smiles kindly, and flashes the nearby picture of her daughter. The technician in the lab—poor soul stuck there on a Saturday—jokes a bit with Nikki and sends her off with a hearty *good luck*.

We head next to Fred Meyers to pick up that one last item: umbilical care diapers. This may be the epitome of commercialism, putting yet another spin on the lowly, primal diaper. But it's thoughtful commercialism, is it not? These itty bitty diapers have a notch cut out at the top, giving the tender, healing stump of the cord respite from undue diaper pressure. It takes a bit of hunting, but we finally find this esoteric item of the diaper world. We glance around the enormous store as if there's something else we must need, but today, there's nothing else to buy Nikki's already stocked the cupboards and fridge for the days ahead. She does pick up a Soaps magazine at the check stand. I stifle an urge to say, "Read it quick, honey."

"When's the baby due?" asks the clerk.

"Day after tomorrow," says Nikki brightly. "Caesarean."

"So this is last-stop shopping, huh?"

"That's right."

"And this is Mom?" she asks, nodding in my direction.

What follows is the quintessential pregnant pause, which I fill by saying, "One of them."

"My mother-in-law," Nikki adds.

Such simple and true words. It's just that in living memory, Nikki has never referred to me that way. In fact, on purpose and by agreement, we'd never exchanged cards with the infamous *law* marring its message. It's not that we're pretending. We both know this is not the same immutable bond as the one she shares with her mother—a bond that would and should, for instance, entitle Ginny to stay with daughter and infant grandson when everyone else departs in a few days. It's just that our friendship, brought to us compliments of a marriage, seemed to deserve something better than traditional vernacular had to offer. So I became Mom easily, and some-times for clarification, "Justin's Mom," or "our Mom." But never mother-in-law. Without the mother-in-law incident of two days before, perhaps this would have been mere surprise, discussed jovially on the way to the parking lot. But no such luxury today. Today, the simple words coagulate in my heart and make a knot. And worst of all, I know I can't hide it from Nikki. The public restroom is my refuge in such a moment.

Nikki and I had decided to indulge in an order of onion rings on the way home. Not ordinary onion rings—the seasonal and colossal rings made from sweet Vidalia onions, deep-fried to perfection by the neighbor-hood Burgerville. While she orders, I duck into the restroom, close myself in a stall (this sounds familiar), and cry. Underneath it all, and in the face of truth-telling hormones and loyal genes, am I really just a mother-in-law after all? Instantly, this insecurity morphs into seeing myself not just as the in-law, but the outsider. All the angst of last December comes spilling back into my heart: all the ways I'm different from Nikki's family, from Brad and Cindy, from the nature of the clan. I could stay in the stall, caught in my emotional down spiral, but I know it will only be a matter of time un-til Nikki comes looking for me. Better to make my exit from a bathroom door than from a stall. There will no hiding the fact that I've been crying, and no evading the scoop unless I flat out refuse to talk about it, which would be the biggest mistake I could make.

I make my way back to the table where a carton of onion rings and Nikki's sympathetic face await me. She's already asking the question before I sit down.

"Mom, what's the matter?"

"I need to talk, honey," I say simply. "I'm really feeling upset, and I know it's no use trying to hide it from you."

And talk I do. About the incident with Jane's friend. About the encoun-ter at the grocery store. "Neither of these is really the issue, Nik. It's just that they bring up that feeling of being different. Mostly I don't mind that, but there are times when I feel like the odd woman out. And then I start feeling very insecure, and begin to pull inside myself. But in two days, my grandson is going to be born and I want to be fully present—not playing some game in my head about being the loner."

She smiles at me and reaches out her hand. "Be yourself, Mom. You're as much a part of this family as anyone else. One of the things I'm grateful for is that the man I love came with a mother we both love."

The knot in my heart starts uncoiling and relief begins to coax my face into a smile. "But don't you find it the least bit weird that the high-on-hormones daughter is offering consolation to the mother who's crying in public?" I ask.

She laughs and squeezes my hand. "I didn't say you aren't strange—I said I love you."

Something happened after that. Something inside of me let go. It was as if I'd come full circle—with the insecurities evoked by Jaden's conception culminating all these months later into deep and intimate confession. That's what the whole spiritual point was, I realized. That was the intent behind the mother-in-law anomalies and the feelings of being less important: to get me to be real over onion rings at Burgerville. To share what I've withheld about my struggle. To go into Grand-motherhood with the greatest possible shot at an open heart.

That Evening

The three of us watch the movie, *The Royal Tenenbaums* tonight, and to a person, we see my Dad in Gene Hackman's character, Royal. Not just a little either. Not like, "You know, he kind of reminds me of Bapa." More like a running commentary of, "Oh my *gosh* he looks like Bapa! That sounds just like Bapa. Go back, go back! Look at that—that could be Bapa!" In the space of those two hours, my father is as present as Royal

Tenenbaum. Even the melancholy tone of this dark comedy seems fitting. For through the medium of this movie, we are not only remembering my Dad with uncanny accuracy, but we are feeling his absence too. His absence on this, the almost-eve of his first great-grandchild's birth. And for me, wide-eyed in the dark that night, it is something more. It feels like my Dad has actually been there, letting us know he is with us, letting us know he is in on the magic.

Modern-Day Magi Arrive with Family-sense and Mirth

July 14

Now, the day after tomorrow has yielded the inevitable prize, and I awake to sun and soul shine. Justin gets up early and goes to church, while Nikki and I sit on the couch in our bathrobes, sipping coffee and watching a video of Celine Dion on Oprah. She sings the title song from her latest CD, *A New Day*—a song about the birth of her long-waited child, a son. Do I need to say that we cry, that we exclaim aloud, that we unlock hands only to wipe tears? And then, in the wake of this moment, Celine announces her upcoming and long-term concert ground: in Las Vegas, where she can reign as both doting mother and world-class performer.

Nikki and I turn to each other and simultaneously say, "We're going."

"Between babies," I add, emphatically. When Justin arrives home a few minutes later, we've rewound to the song and are still huddled together.

"We're going to Las Vegas to see Celine," Nikki tells him joyfully.

"Have a good time," he replies as he rounds the hall corner. His musical tastes run in hard right angles to ours.

We make breakfast at home today: scrambled eggs with all the appropriate trimmings. And then, in a flurry of baby-driven industry, we set to work. I vacuum out the cars and clean the windshields while Justin mows the lawn and works on assembling the playpen. Justin and Nikki spend a

long time brushing the dogs. Cars and lawn and canines must all be in top
form, as if Jaden is going to arrive complete with clip board and want to
do a thorough inspection before he makes his final decision. But of course,
this day-before frenzy isn't for Jaden as much as it is for us. It's communal
nesting, a way to ready ourselves for the thing we still can't quite yet believe. A way to convince ourselves that it's real.

In the afternoon, Nikki and I go to get one final decaf mocha frappe, the
summer treat that has been our ritual over the last few days. To our shock,
and to Nikki's utter dismay, her favorite drive-up is closed. We try another
one close-by, but it's closed too. The jaunt has now become a search, with
the craving of a ready-to-deliver woman at the helm. Our quest takes us
over the back roads to McMinnville, Nikki's former professional stomping grounds. We've called ahead to make sure they're open—and make
frappes. Once the frosty delectables are in hand, I pop out of the car and
take a picture of Nik holding her drink out the window in triumph. Jaden
will like that story.

Back home in the yard, we polish off our drinks in the last of the day's
sunny blessing, and decide on pizza for dinner. She orders, I make salad.
The three of us eat. It's still early, much earlier than we usually eat dinner,
but between the late breakfast and our rush of industry, lunch somehow
didn't make the docket. We putter after dinner—me cleaning up the
kitchen, Justin tending the dogs, Nikki double-checking her suitcase.
Nikki talks to her parents on the phone. They're on their way and will
be here in a few hours. It's just starting to get dark when the three of us
reconvene in the living room and decide to watch some taped episodes
of *Trading Spaces*.

Half-way through the second one, there's a knock on the door. We cock
our heads and frown. It's too early for Sam and Ginny's arrival. "Is someone at the door?" one of us asks aloud, although it's obvious we all heard
the same thing. Justin pauses the TV and gets up, opening the door to

the gathering dark. I can't see who's on the porch, but I see my son open the screen and step out onto the stoop. "Hey!" he exclaims. He's hugging someone. Nikki and I exchange glances and stand up just as Justin leads his Dad and Cindy into the house. "Surprise!" they say, and Nikki and I gasp, then move toward them, arms open. They've come for the birth! *Last night my Dad, tonight Justin's Dad,* I think to myself. *In one way or another, we're all gathering for this life-changing event.* We stand in the middle of the room and pepper them with questions, eliciting their story of deciding to surprise us. "In the end, we just had to come," Brad says by way of summary. "It was not to be missed." His voice is upbeat, but I hear the underlying emotion. I feel joyful, utterly joyful. And when I look at my son's face, I see my joy reflected and magnified. We all gravitate to the nursery then, eager to have Brad and Cindy see the final result of the project they helped launch a couple of months before.

"Did you see Justin's face?" Nikki says to me later, while Justin takes Brad and Cindy for a garage tour of baby accoutrements.

"I did," I say, hugging her, and therefore Jaden, tightly.

"It means so much that they came," she says, tearful.

"It's perfect," I reply. Part of me wishes we could all just cry, just burst into spontaneous, tearful combustion with the heat of our elation. Nonetheless, it's clear what we're all feeling. No one will go to sleep wondering.

About 9 o'clock, Sam and Ginny arrive and the celebration elevates again. Pizza is reheated and passed, wine is poured, strawberry shortcake is prepared. It's an atmosphere that deserves the archaic and undervalued term, *jolly.* As I sit in the glow of this circle, I assume that my Dad's spirit is joining in the delight, and hope that my mother in Boise, Gavin on a venture back east, and Nikki's sister and brother-in-law (who will join us in the morning), are all feeling the radiating quality of our birth-eve party. And I have no doubt that Jaden himself is riding high on the vibration of our laughter and love, our extreme anticipation. We take multiple-camera pictures of each other in various couch formations, with Nikki always perched toward the edge for the sake of her belly. We grin with ease, laugh without effort. We are fools. We are happy fools.

Tomorrow our prince will come.

Eventually Brad and Cindy say goodnight and leave for their motel, tired after a long day of driving. Ginny and Sam follow close behind them. The party is over, but the atmosphere remains. Winding down is in order. We tidy up, milling about the living room and kitchen, tossing comments back and forth about the evening—how spontaneous, how surprising, how much fun. "Maybe that's why Jaden wanted a planned entrance," I say. "So we could all be together and have a party." I said it in jest, but once the words are out, it strikes me: the cesarean not only made tonight possible, but made Brad and Cindy's presence at the birth possible. Maybe even mine. It's not that I'd trade a natural birth for a party—or even for a certain person's presence, including my own. It's just that I have to wonder when something so lively and good, something that feels so right, comes from a choice we wouldn't consciously have made. Trusting that God and Jaden know what they're doing is turning out just fine.

"Want to watch the rest of *Trading Spaces?*" Justin asks, and laughingly, we do. The three of us settle back into our places, just where we sat when a knock on the door sent us into orbit several hours before. More accurately, I should say, we were back in our seats. But not really in the same places. After all, we had all just attended our first child, first grandchild, first great-grandchild baby-eve bash.

Justin brings the dogs in after the show. Sid licks her gratitude. Dakota runs around in circles. When they settle on the floor, Nikki gets down there with them—a brave act in her condition—and tells them she needs to talk to them. Like a good parent, she patiently explains the coming event, and how it is going to mean big changes in their lives. "I'm counting on you to accept your little brother and watch out for him, okay?" Dakota sits in front of her, his head cocked, listening intently. Sid is a harder sell. Despite repeated efforts to engage her, she sits behind Nikki with her back turned. She's hearing, but she isn't listening.

I'm very late to bed, but unable to sleep. So I lie in the dark, remembering when I felt like Sid, reluctant to hear the good news; although unlike Sid, I'd always known that's what it was. Now I'm the image of Dakota: eager and intent, willing and open. I'm tingling and calm at the same time, my senses alert. And even if I don't sleep—or sleep much—it's okay. Here in the stillness, with the feather weight of the sheet over me, I am ready. I may not have claimed my new status quickly or with ease, but here I am. I'm present and accounted for. If there was any turning back to be had, I wouldn't even give it a glance.

This is what matters to me. I didn't want to be one of those but-the-minute people. "But the minute they laid him in my arms …" "But the minute I laid eyes on him …" Nothing really wrong with that, I know; but somehow, it wouldn't have been right for me. It wasn't Jaden's job to help me find the inner grandma and give her a home. It was mine.

"I'm here, dear heart," I say to him in the lull of the crickety night. "I've found my way to you in my own time and by my own means, and I promise you that you are free to do the same with me. As I fly in and out of your life across the months and years ahead, know that I will take you as you are. You don't have to be smiling or clean or ever-sweet. And I promise that I won't let anyone prompt you to kiss me or tell me you love me. That's up to you. In fact, you can decide as much as I do what this relationship will be. I'm not likely to be the traditional Grandma so there won't be as many presents or homemade cookies or new clothes coming from my direction, but on the other hand, I'm pretty good at Silly, have a dramatic reading style, and a fair repertoire of amusing accents and funny faces. I want to share my backyard with its pond and hammock and climbing trees with you. I want to take to you Dillon Beach and to The Sandcastle, my favorite beach house there. I want to give you a big dose of the life that is mine under the California sun.

But most of all, I want to show you myself. The only way I know how to do that is by *being* myself, which isn't always playful and fun. Sometimes I'm sad and scared; sometimes I want to be alone. I hope you'll find out that you can be those ways with me too. The thing is, you're my grandchild and I'm your grandma. But first and foremost, we're just ourselves: Jaden and Maridel sharing the precious, complicated blessing of being alive together.

So let me be the first to say the words you'll hear a hundred times before you're grown: "Get some rest, sweetheart. Tomorrow's a big day. I'll see you in the morning."

July 15

There are only a handful of moments in a lifetime that imprint themselves on your psyche, setting up permanent tableaus, becoming classics that remain while the art of life shifts around you. Here is one of those rare moments:

I'm dressed in yellow and white, standing in a large, sunny room with the green and blue of tree and sky at my back. My focus, like the focus of those around me, is on the corridor that opens from our door. Suddenly, amidst the backdrop of hospital life, a young handsome man in blue scrubs emerges, carrying a newborn child. The arms are strong and protective. The face is lit up from within. The steps are purposeful. It is my firstborn, carrying his first child toward me, toward all of us, and into the evolving story of family and of life.

Jaden Quincy enters the room in the arms of his father, with the pediatrician following close behind. As Justin holds him up to us, then lays him on the little cart, we encircle him, taking in that first heart-stopping gaze, that first breath of his being. My arm goes around Ginny's and hers around me. Collectively, we lean toward our first grandson, smiling effortlessly, tears welling unabashedly. It's true that you can have a holy moment anywhere, and one of ours is here—in the maternity ward of the Providence Hospital in Newberg, Oregon. A moment at once so universal and so personal: when a child that belongs to all of us imprints himself on our hearts forever.

We stay close while the doctor inspects what appears to our eyes to be a perfect being. As we take turns shielding his eyes from the heating lamp above him, he is pronounced "a late breech," meaning that he had settled into his birth posture late in the game, as indicated by the fact that his legs are pulled up only to his hips and not to his ears. *It was a strategic move then,* I think to myself, *arrived at after a fair amount of contemplation.* Either that, or he got stuck one day and decided to sit it out.

Once pronounced healthy, given his eye drops, and bathed by the nurse, Jaden is handed back to his father, who subsequently puts him into my arms. In the weeks prior to his birth, I had read that newborns from other cultures, who traditionally stay with mother and family after birth instead of being ushered off to nurseries, smile spontaneously within an hour of being born. This, in contrast to the six weeks that is customary in our culture. Of course, I'm not thinking of that when Justin gives him to me. I'm not thinking at all. But once settled into my arms, he looks me directly in the eye, holds my gaze, and smiles. Or did I imagine it? What I didn't imagine, though, is that something has passed between us. I'm tempted to call it recognition. Or greeting. Or joy.

Perhaps it is all three.

Epilogues

#1 With a bit of thinly-disguised coaching from his mother, Jaden started called me "Delly" when he was a little over a year old. To my surprise, I found that I liked it; and slowly, it dawned on me why. It also dawned on me where Nikki had first heard it. My friend, Belinda, for undisclosed reasons all her own, had started calling me Delly some years before. She was part of the spiritual community to which I belonged, and yet the name never caught on with anyone else. It was always just Belinda's own. I think she actually stopped thinking of me as Maridel. "I was in the grocery store the other day," she told me once, "and when a voice came over the loudspeaker, 'Deli, you have a call on line one,' I turned to look for you."

So here's the thing: for years, Belinda owned and operated a large, successful housekeeping agency. But I've always thought of it as a front for other, more authentic Belindas. For one, Belinda the Medium, the wild and zany fount of uncanny intuition. Sometimes it came out of her without her knowing it was intuitive at all. And sometimes, she knew … what she knew … what she knew. So what I decided is that, in her prescience, Belinda named me. That she *knew*, before any of the rest of us, that I was a Delly in the making.

#2 One evening when Jaden was a about two-and-a-half, he was playing contentedly in the living room, his mother and I lounging on couches to either side of him. The intricacies of our conversation are no longer remembered, but their content caused Nikki to refer to me as his "grandma." He stopped playing and looked at her in dismay.

"No," he said definitively, "she's not grandma. She's *just* Delly."

Nikki lives to get a rise out of those she loves, and so she countered, "Yes she is. She's your grandma."

At that, he moved toward me, as if in defense of my honor. His voice grew adamant.

"No, she's NOT grandma—she's *just* Delly!"

"You tell her, honey," I said.

My little knight in very shiny *amour.*

#3 I recently picked up a four-year-old Jaden at pre-school. "Delly!" he exclaimed, running toward me with open arms, as if I had at long-last found my way back into his life. In actuality, it had been two-and-a-quarter hours. With arms still around me, he looked up at his teacher and announced, "She's my grandma." I felt myself inwardly startle. Then he released me and started down the hall, but suddenly stopped and looked back at me.

"You are my grandma, right?" he asked.

I burst into an open grin. "That I am, love. That I am."

Afterward

"Grandmotherhood" has been kind to me—I've fallen in love, learned to dance, changed my hair, glamorized my style and—neither last nor least—started to write for a living!

Oh, my grandchild? Well, that *is* a case of saving the best for last.

To me, it's no co-incidence that the birth of Jaden Quincy Bowes was swiftly followed by my own rebirth. The inexpressible, breathing wonder of a first grandchild speaks to your cells … and to your sense of mortality. There you are, further down the line, yet starting all over again. Why not make it spectacular?

Jaden will soon turn seven, and his magical blend of sweetness and fire, his very presence in the world, has cheered me on to live my life less cautiously. I've observed that when he loves something (swimming, fishing or cake), he loves it unreservedly. And when he loves *someone*, he does the same. I'm endeavoring to follow suit—to love with fewer conditions and greater gusto.

But my darling firstborn is no longer a solo act. On St. Patrick's Day three years ago, Abigail arrived! I couldn't have dreamed up a better pair. To his natural sweetness, she is sass. He loves the whole world – she is selective. To his gift for relating, she offers hers: entertainment of self and others. He's a prince and she is most definitely a princess. If you don't happen to notice, she'll tell you.

On my visits to Portland, the three of us walk to the park, watch cartoons, hang out in the backyard, play games and chat in bed. One of my favorite recurring moments is when we're alone in the kitchen at the start of the day, sharing a big platter of peanut butter and celery sticks. We munch to the tune of our own silly, meandering conversation. I like to spend one-on-one time with each of them as well. A movie or shopping excursion with Jaden; a tea party in Abby's room. It changes with every visit, reminding me not only how short the span of childhood is, but how important it is to adapt to the shifting, moon-like phases of a relationship with a child. What's available this visit, may not be the next.

"Come back here and sit with me, Delly," a three-year-old Jaden beckoned from of the back seat of the car. We were in the parking lot of Target waiting for his Mom to complete a quick purchase.

"Oh, Mommy will be right back, honey." I said, thinking that I would only get unstrapped and settled in the back before she would reappear.

"Don't you want to *cuddle*, Delly?"

I almost leapt over the seat.

Grandchildren, I'm learning, are the best teachers of a radical and often unlearned lesson: never miss a chance to love.

Maridel Bowes
Roseville, California
April 2009

About Maridel

Maridel Bowes, M.A. is a professional writer and speaker. According to her mother, she talked before she walked. According to her English teacher, her essays were too long but she couldn't find anything to cut. Yet Maridel has one passion greater than her pursuing her gifts: using them to evoke women's soulfulness, sassiness and spirit.

Out of her experience as a therapist, astrologer and workshop leader, she shakes up a literary cocktail of what's deep, funny and real in women's lives—in the hopes of supporting them to trust their own true light.

Visit Maridel at EvolvingJourney.com and sign up for her newsletters, *Crossing Paths* and *But That's Not All!*